Toxic Relationships is a must ... need for relational wisdom, ... for anyone ... ministry and discipleship. This book reminds us that our hope is not in what people offer, but in what God offers us through the person of his Son, Jesus. I am very grateful for such a biblically rich, helpful resource on such an important topic.

—**Hunter Beless**, Host, *Journeywomen* podcast

Unlike Job, most of us never experience frontal attacks from Satan. Instead, we are worn down by the saturation of our culture and our own hearts with Satan's lies. Lies about God. Lies about ourselves. Lies about how God's world really works. When believed, his lies shrivel our souls, tempt us into toxic relationships, and trap us in life-dominating sins. Ellen Dykas, in *Toxic Relationships*, lovingly and biblically confronts the lies we are so prone to believe with refreshing and liberating truth from the heart of God himself. Read, reflect, and act. You won't be disappointed.

—**Jim Berg**, Professor of Biblical Counseling, Bob Jones University Seminary; Author, *Changed into His Image* and *Quieting a Noisy Soul*; Counsel Member, Biblical Counseling Coalition; Executive Director, Freedom That Lasts

Ever since Adam and Eve shared the forbidden fruit, human relationships have been plagued by sin. Sometimes, sin sets us against one another; other times, it pulls us into unhealthy entanglements. These codependent relationships may seem harmless at the beginning, but their ultimate effect is toxic. If you find yourself—or someone you love—trapped in a toxic relationship, Ellen Dykas's book will be a lifeline. With a counselor's wisdom and a friend's sympathy, Dykas brings readers to passages of Scripture that will expose the flaws in our relationships, explain the deep needs of every human heart, and point again and again to the gracious comfort that can be found in Christ alone.

—**Megan Hill**, Author, *A Place to Belong: Learning to Love the Local Church*; Editor, The Gospel Coalition

Ellen Dykas has given the church a wonderful gift in this latest devotional, walking and working us through toxic relationships. The book begins by reminding us that God is our refuge, and it ends with a hopeful reminder that Jesus is our truest comfort and friend. For those who have been hurt, trapped, and betrayed by toxic relationships, Ellen gives way neither to despair nor dismissal but, like a gentle friend, guides us along a path of healing and restoration. This book will be a balm to the hurting heart.

—**Jonathan D. Holmes**, Founder and Executive Director, Fieldstone Counseling; Pastor of Counseling, Parkside Church, Chagrin Falls, Ohio

Ellen speaks hopeful biblical truths to people who desire to be deeply known and loved yet find themselves hurt and empty in their relationships. Each devotional is filled with tender wisdom, helping you to reorder your relational desires so that you find refuge in the most faithful lover of your soul.

—**Darby A. Strickland**, Counselor, Christian Counseling & Educational Foundation; Author, *Is It Abuse?*

TOXIC
RELATIONSHIPS

31-Day Devotionals for Life

A Series

Deepak Reju
Series Editor

T O X I C
RELATIONSHIPS

TAKING
REFUGE
IN CHRIST

ELLEN MARY DYKAS

PUBLISHING
P.O. BOX 817 • PHILLIPSBURG • NEW JERSEY 08865-0817

Library of Congress Cataloging-in-Publication Data

Names: Dykas, Ellen, 1965- author.
Title: Toxic relationships : taking refuge in Christ / Ellen Mary Dykas.
Description: Phillipsburg, New Jersey : P&R Publishing, [2021] | Series: 31-day devotionals for life | Includes bibliographical references. | Summary: "Are you caught in a relationship that is all-consuming, obsessive, and damaging? Use this devotional to reset your priorities by finding freedom-and lasting security-in Christ and the gospel"-- Provided by publisher.
Identifiers: LCCN 2020052567 | ISBN 9781629957340 (paperback) | ISBN 9781629957357 (epub) | ISBN 9781629957364 (mobi)
Subjects: LCSH: Interpersonal relations--Religious aspects--Christianity--Prayers and devotions.
Classification: LCC BV4597.52 .D95 2021 | DDC 242/.4--dc23
LC record available at https://lccn.loc.gov/2020052567

Contents

Jesus Is the Loving Refuge Who Provides All You Need

How to Nourish Your Soul

A *little bit* *every day* can do great good for your soul.

I read the Bible to my kids during breakfast. I don't read a lot. Maybe just a few verses. But I work hard to do it every weekday.

My wife and I pray for one of our children, every night, before we go to bed. We usually take just a few minutes. We don't pray lengthy, expansive prayers. But we try to do this most every night.

Although they don't take long, these practices are edifying, hopeful, and effective.

This devotional is just the same. Each entry is short. Just a few tasty morsels of Scripture to nourish your starving soul. Read it on the subway or the bus on the way to work. Read it with a friend or a spouse every night at dinner. Make it a part of each day for thirty-one days, and it will do you great good.

Why is that?

We start with Scripture. God's Word is powerful. Used by the Holy Spirit, it turns the hearts of kings, brings comfort to the lowly, and gives spiritual sight to the blind. It transforms lives and turns them upside down. We know that the Bible is God's very own words, so we read and study it to know God himself.

Our study of Scripture is practical. Theology should change how we live. It's crucial to connect the Word with your daily life. Often, as you read this devotional, you'll see the word *you* in the application section because Ellen speaks directly to you, the reader. The readings contain a mixture of reflection questions and practical suggestions. You'll get much more from this experience if you answer the questions and do the practical exercises. Don't skip them. Do them for the sake of your own soul.

Our study of Scripture is worshipful. Relationships are scary and fraught with difficulties. Our insecurities can make us emotionally unstable, overly dependent, and fearful. We get entangled and bogged down in toxic relationships. So, we turn to God's Word. The Scriptures help us to disentangle ourselves from the cobweb of messy relationships and point us to Christ as our everlasting security. People make for insufficient foundations. Build your life around another person, and you will inevitably be hurt and disappointed. We can never get from people the satisfaction that our souls desire. God gives us his Word to reorient our worship away from the people whom we so desperately want, to himself instead. We embrace God's Word because it points us to Christ as our one, true, and sufficient foundation.

If you find this devotional helpful (and I trust that you will!), reread it in different seasons of your life. Work through it this coming month, then come back to it a year from now to remind yourself that our security must ultimately be in Christ.

If, after reading and rereading Ellen's devotional, you want more gospel-rich resources about relationships, she has listed several at the end of the book. Buy them and make good use of them.

Are you ready? Let's begin.

Deepak Reju

INTRODUCTION

Moving toward Your True Refuge

WHAT ARE YOU thinking and feeling as you begin this book? Perhaps it seems like you're hanging on for dear life while thrown about by your relational circumstances. Like Jesus's disciples on the boat in the tumultuous sea in Mark 4:35–41, you are scared, hurting, and fixated on relational waves that are out of control. Maybe someone who came to be like life for you has withdrawn or ended his or her connection to you. Or a family member (your spouse, parent, child) refuses to love and depend on you the way you crave, the way you feel you *need* to make life bearable. Or have you effectively merged your emotional world with a friend and fixate obsessively on that friend?

Have you ever thought something like the following?

- Why hasn't he texted me today?! Is he spending time with someone else? Why wasn't I invited? Am I being replaced?
- I love her so much—I *need* her! If this relationship ends, I don't want to live anymore; life has no meaning without it.
- You make my day, and you have the power to break my day. My heart, stability, sense of being valuable and lovable rise and fall with how much attention you give me. You are me, and I am you. *Don't leave me!*
- I know I'm a bit over the top in how involved I am in my kids' lives, but they need me—I'm their mother! If my marriage is suffering, so what? It never was that great anyway. God gave me these children, and they are my reason for being alive. If they don't need me, I won't exist anymore.
- I just can't understand why my marriage isn't as satisfying as I thought it would be. I mean, isn't it supposed to be the one relationship in my life that meets all my needs? Isn't my spouse supposed to complete me?

Our desire for satisfying and loving relationships is a good one because it is from God (see James 1:17). He is the Creator of relationships, whether in the context of friends, family, ministry, work colleagues, neighbors, and, of course, spiritual siblings in the body of Christ. However, *God never intended for us to turn other people into our primary refuge or home.* God wants us to depend on him, to live under his authority and care, and to grow in satisfaction with his love for us. When we are secure in Christ, our love for the people in our lives can be healthy, holy, and honoring to God. But when love for Christ and obedience to him become secondary to our relationships or aren't a part of them at all, friendships, romantic relationships, mentoring duos, spiritual leader/follower connections, and family relationships can all slide into idolatry.

According to the Bible, whenever something or *someone* sidelines God from our thoughts, desires, and focus, our lives have gotten off track. The toxic nature of these kinds of relationships can be difficult to diagnose because they can feel so, well, *intoxicating!* The emotional buzz or euphoria that often accompanies intense conversations, physical affection, or a person's adoration of us can be addictive. However, a dynamic of "I need your need of me, and you need my need of your neediness" is messy at best and destructive at worst. Instead of helping us to grow and flourish, sinful dynamics in our relationships imprison us. I've had my share of relationships in which my love for and dependency upon God was displaced by my love for a person's need of me or my role in that person's life. I know what it's like to be anxious, fearful, jealous, and insecure when relational terrain suddenly changes and you're left feeling ousted, left behind, and brokenhearted. God has me on a trajectory of growing freedom from interpersonal patterns that were mired down for years in toxic, unholy dependency.

No matter where you are, God is compassionately aware of the circumstances you're in and knows, really knows, what you are feeling. If you are in relational turmoil, are you willing to have the eyes of your heart and mind reoriented toward him? To gaze upon who he is and then begin to diagnose why there is toxicity in one or more of your relationships? To consider who Jesus is and then move toward humbly understanding that when he is in his rightful place in our lives, people will be in theirs?

Come, join me on this journey. Let's be encouraged with a fresh consideration of our loving, safe Refuge and Lord. Let's honestly face our hearts' tendency to crave and seek from others what only Christ can be for us. More than anything, let's be encouraged to grow as worshippers of God who are healthy in all our relationships.

Engage This Journey with Faith-Fueled Realism

As you begin this book, you may struggle to believe God can change your codependent patterns, and perhaps you don't *feel* desirous of change. Are you, however, willing to ask God to work "in you, both to will and to work for his good pleasure" (Phil. 2:13)? Your first step in pursuing spiritual growth is to believe God's Word and to surrender control of your life to him.

Your next step is to have realistic expectations. Most of us want quick, pain-free solutions to our problems, and problematic relationships are no exception! But your desires, interpersonal patterns, and relationships won't change overnight. Instead, repentance brings about directional change—a slow, steady upward trajectory of growth, transformation, and healthiness. What might growth look like?

- Honestly examining your relational world as you go through this devotional.
- Putting space between yourself and a person you realize you are too dependent upon.[1]
- Initiating time with a new friend or an acquaintance— a growth in willingness to engage with other people relationally.

- Engaging with a community of believers through a Christ-centered, biblically faithful local church. God's people are your "household of faith" (see Gal. 6:10), and local churches provide a unique opportunity to cultivate a variety of types and depths of healthy relationships.
- Reading God's Word as a way to know him, love him, and cultivate your relationship with him.
- Longing for God more and more, loving him, and seeking him out as your primary relationship.

The first section of devotional readings offers you an opportunity to engage in a weeklong fast from having your thoughts preoccupied by any one person or relational situation. If you really—I mean, *really*—want to grow toward relational wholeness, you need to freshly focus on the only one who truly meets your needs: God himself!

The second and third sections will help you to understand the factors that contribute to toxic relationships and to identify steps you can take to become healthier. In the fourth section, you will have several days to gaze upon Jesus—the one who is with you throughout this thirty-one-day journey and all the days of growth, obedience, and transformation that lie beyond it.

Our True Refuge Frees Us from Toxic Relational Dynamics

People problems have been around as long as people have existed outside the garden of Eden! You're not alone in this struggle. Many are familiar with the fear, anger, anxiety, discontent, jealousy, and pain that come together when others don't seem to like, love, or respond to them in the way they desire—in the way they're convinced they *need*. Women and men alike have experienced what it's like to feel trapped, even imprisoned, in a relationship that is obsessive and consuming.

That's why, of all the prayers and songs David uttered from his heart as a shepherd, king, military commander, sinner, and chosen one of God, the cry that resonates with me the most is "Bring me out of prison, that I may give thanks to your name! The righteous will surround me, for you will deal bountifully with me" (Ps. 142:7). God has indeed brought me out of relational prisons and allowed me to have healthy, Christ-honoring relationships in my life. Even though I am surrounded by the righteous, I'll never outgrow the need for God to be my Refuge, first love, and source of security.

As we begin this journey, let's ask God to change our desires as we look to Christ.

> Preserve me, O God, for in you I take refuge.
> I say to the LORD, "You are my Lord;
> > I have no good apart from you."
>
> As for the saints in the land, they are the excellent ones,
> > in whom is all my delight.
>
> The sorrows of those who run after another god shall multiply;
> > their drink offerings of blood I will not pour out
> > or take their names on my lips.
>
> The LORD is my chosen portion and my cup;
> > you hold my lot.
> The lines have fallen for me in pleasant places;
> > indeed, I have a beautiful inheritance. (Ps. 16:1–6)

GOD IS OUR MOST TRUSTWORTHY REFUGE

Lord, I struggle to believe that you really can be a safe place for me in the midst of what I'm facing. I am tormented right now as I battle to believe I can truly be free of the mess in my relational world, and specifically my relationship with _____ . I am hurting, angry, lonely, and anxious and ask you to open my heart to see wonderful things in your Word. Help me to believe your words, Lord, and please cause them to soak into my heart, mind, and life. I need you and want to grow in trusting you to lead me, day by day, step by step, to become healthy and holy in my relationships, even as I struggle to know what that looks like. Thank you that I can offer these cries for help through Jesus, the one I belong to and who calls me friend. Amen.

DAY 1

Our Refuge Now and Forever

I love you, O LORD, my strength. The LORD is my rock and my fortress and my deliverer, my God, my rock, in whom I take refuge, my shield, and the horn of my salvation, my stronghold. (Ps. 18:1–2)

AFTER BEING CHASED by enemies and betrayed by people he loved,[1] David begins here: *I love you, Lord.* That isn't always my go-to prayer when relational disappointments leave me feeling frustrated, left out, and hurt! My inner passive-aggressive, pain-avoidant girl nags me to let her *out*. I can stress and turn inward, which usually results in self-pity. Surely I deserve relief, *right, Lord?!* Surely you want *me* to be loved as I want to be loved, *right, Lord?!*

Ouch. How did my relational motivations get so tangled up in *me*? I want to love Jesus and people with a sincere heart. When I'm disappointed, it's easy to forget the most foundational and beautiful truth of my identity—I'm loved and known by God. God's love for me in Christ enables me to love people rather than demand they love me.

When we forget who we are and who God is, it's easy to rush after earthly relationships that seem to promise escape from all pain and disappointment. Sometimes certain people stir a desire in us to have them meet all our needs, soothe our hearts, or save us in some way. Relationships are a good gift, but even the most loving, well-meaning people can't ultimately deliver us from inner pain or provide unfailing love. Not *really*.

David, like us, needed to learn that only the Lord is a constant safe place, a refuge in this life of storms and unexpected relational weather we can't control. Look at his descriptions of the Lord: *my strength, my rock, my fortress, my deliverer, my shield, my stronghold.*

David's use of the word *my* brings a personal and specific touch to his heartfelt cries. The Lord isn't only *the* most trustworthy refuge; he is *your* and *my* faithful shelter.

Do you turn to the Lord for help regarding your relational struggles, or do you look elsewhere? God is our safe harbor in our relational storms. He changes our hearts to love him more than we love what people can give to us. He is tender toward us when we're weary, unsure if we can really overcome long-held unhealthy relational patterns. Even when we forsake him and insist on seeking security in the companionship and attention of people, the Lord doesn't tire of pursuing us. Unlike weak and sinful humans, his bandwidth for loving us is unfailing and inexhaustible!

I love you, Lord. Turn toward him and begin here today. Through Christ, God delivers us from unhelpful (and unholy) patterns in our relationships and strengthens us to trust him.

Reflect: Later in Psalm 18, David's heart gushes with thankfulness. "He rescued me from my strong enemy . . . for they were too mighty for me" (v. 17). "He brought me out into a broad [spacious, wide] place . . . because he delighted in me" (v. 19). God rescued David because he delighted in him, just as he delights to help you in the relational storms of your life. Christ is with you as you begin this journey!

Act: Pray for God to help you to look to him as your true Refuge, perhaps with words like these: "Lord Jesus, help me to love you and to say no to my false saviors. Strengthen me to say yes to you. Help me to trust in you to deliver me from my relational prisons and to bring me into a safe place of resting and trusting in you. Amen."

DAY 2

Our Heart Healer

*The LORD is near to the brokenhearted and saves
the crushed in spirit. (Ps. 34:18)*

He heals the brokenhearted and binds up their wounds. (Ps. 147:3)

HAVE YOU EVER heard of a wound-care specialist? I have a
friend who is a nurse and spends her days traveling to people's
homes to assess and treat their wounds. She cleans, bandages,
and uses antibiotics to promote healing in bodies that have been
bruised, punctured, and cut.

But what about wounded hearts? How can they be assessed,
bandaged, and healed? Toxic relationships can wound and break
our hearts. We can be crushed by those who manipulate us to
meet their needs. When we become obsessively attached to
someone, believing that person is all we ever need, a betrayal can
devastate our dream of unfailing love.

Scripture uses the word *broken* to describe what happens
when our soul, the center of our will and spiritual life, has been
"shattered, smashed, burst into pieces."[1] The "wounds" that
Psalm 147:3 describes refer to injury, hurt, or pain in someone's
soul. God is compassionately aware of how you carry scars from
sin committed against you. Fools, sinners, and messy people have
made choices that have impacted your life. Betrayal, abandon-
ment, and deceit are not small offenses in God's eyes; he sees you
and knows if you have been on the receiving end of painful, perhaps even traumatic, experiences.

God, our Redeemer and Healer, is the only one who can heal
your heart. In fact, when Jesus began his public ministry, he quoted
Isaiah 61 to describe his ministry, which includes the healing of

broken hearts; this is one of his stated purposes for why his Father sent him into this world (see Luke 4:18–20). Wound-care specialists can treat our physical bodies, yet only God can heal the unseen parts of us. Inside us, where God alone dwells (see Col. 1:27), the Spirit of Christ comforts and heals our pain and grief.

Sometimes our hearts can be wounded by our own sin and idolatry (see Ps. 16:4). Foolish choices, sinful behaviors, and messy relationships bring consequences that expose our dependence upon God not only for forgiveness but for comfort and healing. Our gracious Savior not only delivers us from our sin but also heals and restores us from the consequences of our sin and the sin of others! Yes, we may bear the consequences of foolish sinful choices. Yes, soul-wounding sin done *against us* may produce scars we carry throughout this earthly life. However, Christ's ministry to bandage and heal broken hearts is real!

A healed heart grows by looking to God more—and to people less—for comfort and affirmation. A healed heart can celebrate the sweetness of connection with a friend, spouse, or mentor as a good gift. A heart heals gradually as we allow God's Word and love to wash our wounds, one truth at a time.

Reflect: Does your heart feel broken and bruised? Can you express to God your need for healing in the innermost places of your being?

Act: What consequences of sin—either your own or someone else's—have produced the most painful grief in your life? Many of us bear the scars from obsessive relationships, sexual sin, and selfish actions. Our God of peace can sanctify us completely so that our whole spirit, soul, and body will be kept sound and blameless when Jesus, our heart healer, returns (see 1 Thess. 5:23)! Turn to him now, asking for the mercy and help you need.

DAY 3

The One Who Saves
Us from Ourselves

He has delivered us from the domain of darkness and
transferred us to the kingdom of his beloved Son, in whom we
have redemption, the forgiveness of sins. (Col. 1:13–14)

THERE ARE DAYS when I am compelled to cry out to God with desperation, "Lord, please protect people from me today!" When I am feeling impatient, frustrated, or self-righteous, the people who come in contact with me are in danger if I don't receive God's gracious intervention to change my heart's desires and demands.

I didn't always pray this way. When I was in the throes of fierce relational mess and confusion, the biggest problem I thought I had wasn't located *in* my heart; no, the problem was other people. They weren't delivering on what I assumed they should give to me, and they needed to step up with consistent attention and affirmation. They needed to keep me as a priority—better yet, as their *top* priority! After all, I'd given so much to my relationships, sacrificing so much time and energy for them.

Have you been there? Your spouse, boyfriend, girlfriend, or friend just won't give you what you desperately want, and you're consistently frustrated, disappointed, and hurt. Michael was like that. His wife, Jackie, *was* loving and devoted to him, yet she loved God more than she loved her husband. She talked about the peace and love she experienced in her relationship with Jesus. Michael secretly—and guiltily—felt angry about this. Sure, we need to be serious about God and all that, but she was his wife! Wasn't she supposed to keep him as her number one, the focus of her day, and always consider how to make him feel loved, important, and respected? His biggest problem, or so he thought, was his wife's inability to satisfy his emotional desires. He was blind to the insecurity that contributed to the demands he placed on Jackie to make himself feel secure.

Michael, like me, had allowed his pain and sinful heart's demands to imprison him, and he needed to be delivered. He needed to realize that he had a refuge in the Beloved Son who alone could free him from sin, satisfy his heart, and enable him to love his wife selflessly. The darkness of his heart's secret anger could be transformed with the light of God's kingdom through Jesus, freeing him to let Jackie off the hook from his self-imposed mini-messiah role for her.

God saves us from ourselves—from our sin, selfishness, disordered desires, and skewed priorities. His rescue comes through the person of Jesus, the Beloved Son. Jesus was disappointed, mistreated, unloved, and abandoned, yet he never sinned against those who hurt him. What a comfort that he rescues us *into* himself—as an unfailing friend, spouse, and companion with whom we'll live forever.

Reflect: Have you ever thought that your biggest problem was a person's response or lack of response to you? How have you allowed your focus to shift from asking God to change *your* heart to demanding that he change *someone else* to do or be what you want him or her to be?

Reflect: Have you ever cried out to God to save you from your selfishness and sin and to deliver you into the kingdom of Jesus? If not, pray and ask God to help you to believe that his loving rescue is what you need most.

DAY 4

Our Merciful and Comforting Father

Blessed be the God and Father of our Lord Jesus Christ, the Father of mercies and God of all comfort, who comforts us in all our affliction, so that we may be able to comfort those who are in any affliction, with the comfort with which we ourselves are comforted by God. (2 Cor. 1:3–4)

SHAME. EMBARRASSMENT. What discouraging words do you connect with the confusing relational tendencies you've noticed in yourself? I've met many men and women who describe their struggles with codependency and toxic relationships as *humiliating, stupid,* or *childish.* Many adults fight hidden, painful battles with basing their sense of well-being on a person and that person's responses to them. They secretly feel like the kid sitting alone at lunch in middle school or the only one not on the invite list for the prom party.

Whatever words describe your experiences, you have a God who not only understands but is merciful, gentle, and eager to comfort your heart. His comfort may not seem like what you want most right now, but I guarantee it's what you need.

Because of sin's devastation, there are plenty of ways for our hearts to experience affliction. Emotional distress, fear, and loneliness are afflictions we sometimes face because of relationships. When we get honest about working on our sinful contributions to our relationships, it becomes obvious why we need a rescuing Savior, a counseling Spirit, and a merciful Father! We are a weak and needy people.

Recognizing our weakness and affliction, Paul starts his letter to the Corinthians with a reminder about who God is and what he provides. He is a Father of mercy—he is tenderly aware of what we face in a sinful world. He does not condemn or shame us for our struggles but instead invites us to draw near to him *with* our hurt. He is the God of not some but *all* comfort.

You see, we need to know that God is merciful and comforting when sinful, enslaving desires threaten to rule our hearts in response to pain and disappointment. He assures us of his presence in the midst of what we are feeling. When we are tempted to respond sinfully to difficult relationship situations, God's comfort rescues and settles us. A verse speaks specifically to our heart; someone unexpectedly checks in with caring words; God enlivens faith within us, enabling us to believe that as difficult as our situation is, his love is a sure refuge for us.

Unhealthy relational patterns don't form overnight, and they won't be overcome in a day. Be patient with this process; you are in good hands that are full of comfort.

Reflect: God's mercy and comfort are not distant promises but are available to us today, for our heavenly Father has promised to give us what we need. What kinds of encouragement do you need today? Are there ways you long for comfort? Ponder the promises of 2 Corinthians 1:3–4—the merciful God of all comfort not only can comfort you in all of your pain but also lovingly desires to do so. Remarkable, isn't it? He really does care for us!

Act: God's comfort is a gift that keeps on giving: as we receive his love, he gives us the resources to comfort others in turn. Is there someone in your life who seems to need comfort? It might feel like the last thing you want to do, but there is peace and freedom that comes to us as we offer kindness, regardless of how another appreciates it or reciprocates. God's supply of comfort will never run dry!

DAY 5

Our Helpful Counselor

"If you love me, you will keep my commandments. And I will ask the Father, and he will give you another Helper, to be with you forever, even the Spirit of truth." (John 14:15–17)

IN THE MIDST of a relational struggle, I was feeling uneasy, hurt, and confused. As I discussed it with a friend, she made a gentle suggestion: "Why can't you just tell the person how you feel, Ellen?!"

"That's the point . . . I don't know how!"

My reply caught my well-meaning friend off guard. Ironically, she didn't know how to express what *she was feeling* in response to my admission!

When we struggle to find words for internal angst and pain, we have a Helper, the Holy Spirit. Jesus knew that his followers didn't have the capacity to figure out life, relationships, obedience, suffering, and so on. His solution? He asked his Father (our Father too!) to give them a gift—the Holy Spirit, who is our Counselor, Helper, and Guide. In a mysterious way, God ministers to our hearts through the Spirit.

Over the years, I've grown in self-awareness and learned how to discern how my heart responds to circumstances. Maybe like me, you've read books, talked to wise friends, or visited counselors about your relational struggles. As much as these are helpful steps to take, all growth, including growth in relational wholeness, is enabled by the Holy Spirit, the very life of God living within us.

Jesus encouraged his followers, fearful people who were prone to running from tough circumstances, to "not be anxious about how you should defend yourself or what you should say, for the Holy Spirit will teach you in that very hour what you ought to say" (Luke 12:11–12). How can the Spirit help you when you don't know what to say or don't know why you feel the way you do? Why certain relationships seem prisonlike and oppressive rather than loving and free? You talk to God, asking him to counsel you through the Holy Spirit:

- Lord, help me! I'm scared. . . . I can't imagine letting go of this person, of not having daily contact. Help me to understand why I'm so dependent on her.
- God, my thoughts are spinning, swirling in the orbit of what he said to me. Please guide me into right thinking in this situation, through the mind of Christ.
- Father, I don't have a clue why I'm so obsessed and controlled by what _____ thinks about me. Show me what's true!

Jesus promised not to leave us as orphans but to come to us through the Holy Spirit (see John 14:18). In any given situation, we have a Counselor and Helper to guide us as we call out to him in dependence and trust.

Act: When relationships cloud our view of God, we often don't go to him for the wisdom and guidance we need. Bring any current relational confusion or questions you have to God in prayer, asking the Spirit to counsel you.

Act: David prayed an amazing truth that you need too: "Your testimonies are my delight; they are my counselors" (Ps. 119:24). Ask God to give you a humble heart to receive his counseling as you walk through this book.

DAY 6

Our Loving Lord and Creator

*For by him all things were created, in heaven and on earth, visible
and invisible, whether thrones or dominions or rulers or authorities—
all things were created through him and for him. And he is before
all things, and in him all things hold together. (Col. 1:16–17)*

KARI AND GRACE were the best of friends and gushed with
thankfulness over finding a soul-friend. They connected so easily
and in a short amount of time were amazed at how merged their
lives were. It soon became their norm to text obsessively throughout each day, sharing prayer needs, asking for advice about most
areas of life, and comforting each other when life felt challenging.
When Kari's husband expressed concern about how consumed
Kari was with her new bestie, she angrily defended herself: "I
need her! Her friendship gives me something that you just can't
as a man!"

What had happened? In short, Kari and Grace had given each
other power and control over their lives as they grew addicted
to constant connection and long emotional conversations pow-
ered by their desires to feel loved and needed. Functionally, they
placed their friendship in the control seat of their lives, allow-
ing it to make or break their day, sense of emotional well-being,
and security. Even though both were Christians, God became an
afterthought as they considered each other as the most important part of their lives. No human can carry that burden, and God
alone is to govern our lives!

You see, all really does mean *all*: all things were created
through and for Jesus. This includes every single one of our relationships. Kari and Grace walked into the familiar trap of forgetting that their friendship belonged to God. Kari's marriage and

27

her friendship with Grace were gifts to be enjoyed with Christ at the center, but she made her desire to feel loved her focus.

Many of us want a free pass from Christ's lordship regarding our relationships and desires. We think, "God, you know how lonely I am. What's wrong with having a person be the most important aspect of my life?" or "But her touch is electrifying to me in a way my husband's isn't; I need her!" or "If my wife isn't attentive to me, I'm destroyed; why did God let me marry her if she can't meet all my needs?"

Sound familiar?

When we surrender to Christ's loving lordship over our relationships, we have a safe place from which to enjoy and to love people freely. When we believe that he created us for himself, we can rest knowing he is overseeing our relational world, who's in it and who's not. We will still experience pain and discontent in our relationships from time to time, but rather than sinking into despair, we can draw near to Jesus.

In Colossians 1:18, Paul teaches us that God has given Jesus the first place, or the supremacy, in *everything*. This means that we need to grow in trusting him to be our priority relationship, the one from whom we most seek comfort, direction, and purpose for our lives. Only Jesus, Lord and Creator, who set in motion a beautiful ministry of redemption when he created us, fills all things, including our hearts (see Eph. 1:23).

Reflect: Do you need to let someone off the hook of being what only Jesus can be? It's difficult to let go of the dream that someone will fill your heart. Jesus understands your struggle and will help you to believe that his allness is enough.

Act: If you're in a relationship that controls you in toxic ways, take time to pray that God, your loving Lord, will guide you in giving him control instead.

DAY 7

Our Eternal Source of Spousal Love

"And I will betroth you to me forever. I will betroth you to me in righteousness and in justice, in steadfast love and in mercy. I will betroth you to me in faithfulness. And you shall know the LORD." (Hosea 2:19–20)

FOR YEARS I'VE led biblical support groups for hundreds of wives whose marriages have been impacted by their husbands' sexual unfaithfulness.[1] When years of secret pornography use or adultery come to light, a fractured marriage foundation is usually also exposed.

The tragic stories of deception and the enslaving power of sin vary, but two consistent threads run through most of the wives' stories. First, these excruciating circumstances expose varying degrees of how these wives have looked to their husbands for what only God can provide; suffering often reveals where our hopes are truly set. Second, through these circumstances, the wives grow much closer to the Lord and understand more deeply what it means that he is their Spouse. Over and over again, these women amaze me with their humble acknowledgment of their own sin (idolizing their husbands) and renewed hunger for the Lord.

Through circumstances they would never choose for themselves, these wives bear witness to a beautiful theme in Scripture: God's plan to pursue an eternal marriage relationship with his people. In Hosea, we hear God's desire to be more than just friends, more than a king with servants, even more than a father with his children: he pursues us, loves us, and offers us eternal marriage, with *himself.*

Married to God? Yes! His spousal love is different from human marriage but no less intimate. We have an eternally secure, forever-together relationship bought for us by the blood of Jesus our Bridegroom (see John 3:28–29).

Paul described what's at stake when we pursue anything, including other relationships, over our marriage to Christ. As a spiritual father to the Corinthians, he reminded them that they belong to one husband, Christ, to whom they were to be devoted with sincerity and purity of heart (see 2 Cor. 11:1–3). Perhaps you've allowed a friendship to distract you from God; perhaps you're even seeking spouse-like attention from someone you're not married to. Emotional enmeshment, fused lives, and obsessive keeping tabs on each other can all be subtle ways to turn a same-sex friendship or dating or mentoring relationship into a mini-marriage.

God is jealous for us but not because he feels threatened! He has wedded himself to us, and we belong to him. He loves us too much to allow our hearts to be captivated by his good gifts and in holiness will not allow there to be any gods before him in our lives. As our faithful, eternal Spouse, he chases us day after day with his unfailing love, the holy love he designed our souls to desire.

Reflect: *I am yours, Jesus, and you are mine!* Say it aloud. Pray about it. Ponder it in your heart. You belong to the Savior, the one before whom every knee will bow in adoration (see Phil. 2:9–11) and the Bridegroom who will bring his bride (the church) into the fullness of our marriage with him (see Rev. 19:6–8).

Act: God wants the eternal reality of being *his* to change the way we respond to life. What's one step you can take this week to cultivate your understanding of being a part of the bride of Christ? Review today's Scripture passages, and ask God to help you to understand and believe this aspect of the Christian life.

THE FOUNDATION OF TOXIC RELATIONSHIPS

"The soul . . . craves fulfillment from things outside itself and will embrace earthly joys for satisfaction when it cannot reach spiritual ones. The believer is in spiritual danger if he allows himself to go for any length of time without tasting the love of Christ and savoring the felt comforts of a Savior's presence. When Christ ceases to fill the heart with satisfaction, our souls will go in silent search of other lovers."

John Flavel, *The Method of Grace*

DAY 8

People Idolatry

Every good gift and every perfect gift is from above, coming down from the Father of lights, with whom there is no variation or shadow due to change. (James 1:17)

"You shall have no other gods before me." (Ex. 20:3)

PETER AND LYNN considered themselves loving, sacrificial parents and often told their daughter Emma that they would do anything for her. They called her daily, regularly offered her financial assistance (even though Emma's job generously provided for her), and expected her to spend at least one night of every weekend back home. In short, they hovered over and smothered Emma's attempts to be independent. They couldn't let go of their daughter and frequently reminded her that she was their "most precious gift and priority."

Peter and Lynn were correct: Emma was a gift. However, their style of parenting was an expression of idolatry, a mishandling of our Father's gifts. They had made Emma a mini-god in their lives, depending on her to make them feel good about themselves. Emma was exhausted and confused by her parents' demand that she find life through them.

God is a generous giver of gifts, but the Bible is clear that none of God's gifts are to be exalted over obedience and love for him. He has said, "You shall have no other gods before me." He doesn't demand our exclusive devotion because he is insecure! No, he is a loving Father with a wise design for how his good gifts are to be enjoyed. People and relationships can be among the sweetest blessings we experience on earth, but they make lousy gods. To get gifts and gods mixed up is a recipe for disaster.

What do you value in your relationships? Are you looking to fix someone's life or have someone put your life back together when you feel broken? Is your heart empty and you want someone to make it whole? You run the risk of looking to a person for your value, identity, and security—things only God can give you. This idolatry may be mutual or primarily one-sided, but the common factor of such relationships is that they don't involve a mutual dependence on God.

It's humbling to consider how sinful dynamics develop in our relationships. In the absence of believing and experiencing the truth of who God is as our Refuge, we often default to strategizing and attempting to deliver ourselves from internal pain by finding a person who will satisfy our cravings. You may currently be in a relationship that feels like a prison—you may feel hopelessly addicted to a person and that person's responses to you. Though *idolatry* may be a hard word to swallow in regards to your relationships, God can help you to break the chains that bind you to sinful patterns. Through Christ, you have a gift that will never be taken away: the sure hope of his presence and his power to help you to escape the entanglement and walk free!

Reflect: Have you ever considered how a person can become an idol or mini-god in your life? How we can functionally become relationship addicts? Ask God to show you how these dynamics may be in play in your life.

Act: Reread the Scripture passages above, and ponder how God's command to "have no other gods" in our lives can comfort and protect us in our relationships.

DAY 9

Suffering

Now he was teaching in one of the synagogues on the Sabbath. And behold, there was a woman who had had a disabling spirit for eighteen years. She was bent over and could not fully straighten herself. (Luke 13:10–11)

THE "BENT OVER" woman had a broken body and needed help for a condition she had no control over. Maybe your battle with obsessing about certain relationships or craving someone's attention feels like that. You don't know why you seem bent toward needing certain people's love and attention in order for life to feel worthwhile. You feel hopeless and helpless like this woman, "bent over" in your patterns of relationships, and unsure why or how you got here.

Sydney felt that way. Eric, her pastor, had kindly offered to help her when she confessed a secret life of sexual promiscuity. One guy after another enjoyed her body while she reveled in male attention. It felt so good to be wanted and needed! She'd learned this from her mom, who had frequently had men stay the night while Sydney grew up. Now that she was a Christian, she knew that sex with these guys was wrong but couldn't shake her craving to be wanted.

Sydney and Eric's lives converged when they were both vulnerable. She had just heard again, "I don't want a relationship, but text me if you want to have fun like we did last night!" Eric was in the throes of circumstances mostly outside his control: the elders of his church were never satisfied and consistently critical, while his wife suffered with chronic depression and anxiety and barely engaged her husband. Sydney clung to Eric's pastoral care, rehearsing his words repeatedly in her mind. Eric found reasons to text her almost daily, because "she needs encouragement, and

I'm her pastor, after all." Eric's longing to be validated and Sydney's desperation to be cared for formed a toxic recipe: a mutually emotionally dependent relationship. Both chose to respond sinfully to suffering and the sin done against them as they each allowed their relationship to be fueled by selfish rather than Christ-honoring motivations.

Unhealthy patterns of dependency don't grow out of nowhere. Suffering and pain come at us in ways we cannot control. The trials of life can teach us to fend for ourselves relationally and to not trust people, or to dependently and desperately attach ourselves to certain people. Some women and men have developed deep patterns of insecurity in response to miserable or absent care from key adults in their lives as they were growing up. These childhood patterns continue into adulthood, making a mess of friendships, marriages, and parenting and work relationships.

Jesus not only saves us from our sin but also knows that this sinful world and Satan himself move against us to bruise and break us. Like he did with the woman in today's story, he sees us, calls us to himself out of our current relational location, and speaks words of healing, protection, and celebration over us. He calls sin *sin*, yet he is willing to heal our "weak and wounded, sick and sore" hearts.[1] Will you respond to his call to draw near?

Reflect: In what ways do you feel weak and wounded, sick and sore, bruised and broken, because of living in a fallen world with sinful people?

Reflect: In what ways can you recognize how painful experiences shaped your understanding of how relationships are supposed to work? How is God pointing out sin that you need to repent of as well as a broken heart he wants to heal?

DAY 10

Disordered Desires

"If your brother, the son of your mother, or your son or your daughter or the wife you embrace or your friend who is as your own soul entices you secretly, saying, 'Let us go and serve other gods,' . . . you shall not yield to him or listen to him, nor shall your eye pity him, nor shall you spare him, nor shall you conceal him." (Deut. 13:6, 8)

ENTERTAINMENT AND GREETING cards frequently communicate that other people can fulfill our craving for unfailing, never-disappointing love. The promise of a friend who satisfies all your emotional desires. A romantic and sexual relationship that gives you unwavering purpose and identity. A popular yard sign proclaims, "Love is love," promoting the idea that you can define love by whatever makes you feel loved or loving. That's your truth, so go for it.

The Bible makes it clear that truth, including true love, comes from the true God! "By this we know that we love the children of God, when we love God and obey his commandments. For this is the love of God, that we keep his commandments. And his commandments are not burdensome" (1 John 5:2–3). We love God through our obedience (which includes loving him!) and love people by faithfully living out God's commands.

When our desires are *disordered*, our understanding of love becomes confused. It can feel good to be the focus of someone's worshipful infatuation, yet this intoxication leaves us unfulfilled and ultimately brokenhearted. That's what sin does. Like the Israelites to whom Moses spoke today's verses, we can succumb to the temptation to allow the gift of relationships to replace God in our lives; idolatry is at work when our desires lead us away from God rather than toward devotion to him. Unconscious beliefs, such as the following, can leave us with desires that don't align with God's Word:

- My emotional and sexual attractions are my compass for true love.
- We're each other's number one: I'm all into you, and you're into me; I'm your person, and you're mine.
- As long as I can take care of you, I know you love me; meeting your needs gives me purpose.

Godly love is not burdensome or boring! It is freeing, joyful, and peace-infusing; it enables us to love others faithfully and to receive love healthily. Disordered desires are transformed through Christ's dwelling within us through his Spirit. Though our natural desires are corrupt and sinful (see 2 Peter 1:4), God supernaturally gives us the new desires of the Spirit, who transforms our relationships (see Gal. 5:17).

Reflect: Jude wrote a letter to help believers to stand strong against false teaching, saying, "But you, beloved, building yourselves up in your most holy faith and praying in the Holy Spirit, keep yourselves in the love of God, waiting for the mercy of our Lord Jesus Christ that leads to eternal life" (vv. 20–21). How can this help you to resist the "love is love" message?

Act: If today's reading hits home for you, consider offering this as a humble cry for help: "God, show me how to live in your love more than I seek to live in my desires for the love of people. I want to develop a lifestyle of obedient love that produces healthy, meaningful connections with people, because I'm deeply connected to you. Amen."

DAY 11

Misplaced Hope

*Because your steadfast love is better than life, my lips will praise
you. . . . My soul will be satisfied as with fat and rich food, and
my mouth will praise you with joyful lips. (Ps. 63:3, 5)*

*May the God of hope fill you with all joy and peace in believing, so that
by the power of the Holy Spirit you may abound in hope. (Rom. 15:13)*

IT'S COMMON TO place ultimate hope in people and what
they offer us more than hoping and trusting in God. We want to
feel that we are known deeply and loved perfectly; we desire to be
irreplaceable to someone and hope they feel the same about us.
However, when we search for ultimate meaning in earthly relationships rather than in God, we've misplaced our hope.

David's worshipful words in Psalm 63 about God's satisfying love reveal where his hope was placed and are astounding
when we consider the relational world of the "man after [God's]
heart" (1 Sam. 13:14). He had multiple wives, a kindred spirit
friendship with Jonathan (see 1 Sam. 18:1), and a prophet of
God who invested in him so that he'd be faithful to the Lord (see
2 Sam. 12:1–15). In all these relational scenarios, the ultimate
outcome in David's life was reveling in *God and the hope he had
in him;* it was God's love that he considered supremely satisfying.

David had it right: our hope needs to be focused on God's
unwavering, soul-satisfying, steadfast love. People can indeed
image God's love—which is a beautiful gift—yet our ultimate
hope for satisfaction should be not in what people offer us but in
the One who gives the gift of relationships in the first place.

Imagine what can happen when we begin the day praying as
David did: *Lord, fill my heart and satisfy me with your love today.*

Our friendships will be enjoyable and a source of encouragement when we don't place our hope in their being our all in all. Our spouses can be comforted and blessed by our love when Christ our Bridegroom is our ultimate prize. The respect of your children and your importance to them become things to pray about rather than demand by attempting to satiate their every whim.

The Bible gives examples of meaningful, mutually encouraging relationships that kept the God of all hope, not the relationship itself, at their center. Jonathan and David were knit in spirit for the Lord's glory and their good (see 1 Sam. 18:1–3; 20:12–17). Elizabeth and Mary magnified the Lord together, rejoicing in his miraculous acts (see Luke 1:39–45). Paul and Timothy, close companions and spiritual family for each other, kept love for Christ as their bond (see 2 Tim. 1:1–7). Paul pastored people by pointing them first to the grace, love, and peace of God our Father and the Lord Jesus Christ. He expressed deep love for his congregations, yet his letters never give a sense that his hope was dependent on their responses to him.

If you've placed your hope on what people can give rather than on God, have hope! The very One we may have inadvertently displaced with a person will never withhold his love or displace us.

Reflect: How much do you hope, and perhaps demand, that people be what only God can be for you: a perfect source of love, affirmation, and never-failing commitment? How is God gently drawing you to himself, while leading you away from those misplaced hopes?

Act: Take today's verses and consider praying them daily for the next week. Ask God to reorient your heart's hope onto himself.

DAY 12

Unbelief

Without faith it is impossible to please him. (Heb. 11:6)

*Trust in the LORD with all your heart, and do not lean on
your own understanding. In all your ways acknowledge him,
and he will make straight your paths. (Prov. 3:5–6)*

HAVE YOU EVER considered how your faith is a key factor in
the nature of your relationships? The main idea of Hebrews 11 is
that God's people must live by faith; in fact, without faith we can't
please God!

When we depend on our own wisdom and don't believe what
is true about God, life, ourselves, and all things relational, unbelief is at work. Solomon's words in our second reading today urge
us to anchor our understanding of everything, including relationships, not in ourselves but in God and his truth. Toxic relationships always have unbiblical, self-determined convictions and
strategies, or unbelief, at their core. We think (believe) that we
deserve to be loved the way we want and demand that people
make us feel good about ourselves. We are convinced (believe)
that a deep connection with someone who becomes a god to us
is actually a beautiful commitment. We believe ourselves over the
gospel—which disciples us to love God above all else, to have no
gods before him in our lives, to love people selflessly with honor,
dignity, and care rather than using people to soothe our hearts.

Solomon is an example of someone who, like us, believed
in God yet gave way to unbelief as well. He trusted in his own
understanding rather than God's commands and experienced the
painful consequences in many ways, including in his relationships
(see 1 Kings 11:1–13). However, we can use the wisdom Solomon gained to fight unbelief with the Word of Life.

Consider taking the following steps:

- *Pray* that you will believe what God says about friendship, love, relational desires, and so on. Unbiblical beliefs you've had, which have been borne out in patterns of codependency, obsessive attachment, and an inability to implement boundaries with people, can be changed. He can cause your faith in what is true to grow!
- *Turn away* from worldly thinking, such as "This is just the way I am; I can't do relationships differently," and *turn toward* what Scripture promises about your identity in Jesus and how he transforms us.
- *Acknowledge your need* of God and his Word to shepherd you in every relationship.
- *Place your hope* in his ability to transform your relational paths into life-giving, healthy connections with others.

Solomon's father, King David, prayed, "Search me, O God, and know my heart! Try me and know my thoughts! And see if there be any grievous way in me, and lead me in the way everlasting!" (Ps. 139:23–24). Just like Solomon and David, we can ask God to search us out and to reveal to us the ways in which we've believed and acted on worldly thinking rather than the gospel. We can grow in believing what is true about ourselves as new creations in Christ (see 2 Cor. 5:16–17). This is biblical self-awareness grounded in faith that can lead to relational freedom and joy!

Act: Read Psalm 139. God knows you better than you know yourself and will help you to believe what is true.

Reflect: Now that you're nearly halfway through this devotional, what have you learned about wrong beliefs you've held regarding God and relationships with people?

HOW TO PURSUE
RELATIONAL HEALTH

Lord, it's comforting to know that you understand that change can be painful. I don't always feel it, but I want to grow to rest in the truth that you are my true Refuge. I want to step forward in growth, to trust you in ways I've probably never done before. I don't know what the road in front of me looks like, but I want to depend on you and believe what David said: "You are my Lord; I have no good apart from you." I want to grow in having people in their rightful place in my life, my heart, and my desires; I don't want to use people anymore but to learn how to love them because I'm loved and secure in you, Lord. I don't want to be bound up in fear and insecurity based on how people need or want me, but I do desire deep, caring relationships. Change me, Lord! Help me to walk forward, one step at a time, trusting in you and believing that obedience is worth it. Amen.

DAY 13

Ask God to Reveal Your Heart's Pain and Sin

Search me, O God, and know my heart! Try me and know my thoughts! And see if there be any grievous way in me, and lead me in the way everlasting! (Ps. 139:23–24)

IT CAN BE hard to figure out why certain people hook us emotionally or why we can't seem to shake an unhealthy attachment to someone. When someone isn't paying attention to us in the way we want, our emotional turmoil can morph into screaming pain; figuring out what to do with it is overwhelming. Scripture encourages us to acknowledge to God what's happening inside our hearts and to receive his comfort and help.

Let's unpack today's verses to understand how to confess the pain and sin lurking in our hearts. David's final words in this famous psalm show us how to do it. He asks God for several things.

- *Search and know me*: Father, explore every crevice of my heart and mind. Help me to understand what I'm feeling. I won't keep avoiding you, Lord . . . reveal the real deal of my heart to me!
- *Try me and know my thoughts*: God, I need you to examine why I'm anxious, fearful, hurting so much. Am I self-deceived about this relationship? Am I blind to the real causes of my anger, fear, jealousy, and insecurity?
- *See any grievous way in me:* Lord, humble me and show me what sinful patterns are in my life. What paths of pain have I made for myself?
- *Lead me in your ways*: Good Shepherd, I need you to guide me and to give me your comfort and the spiritual wisdom

I lack. Help me to receive what you show me, Lord, even if it's ugly and scary. Give me a teachable and leadable heart to trust and follow you.

Friend, God's "way everlasting" most likely will begin a new season of grief. *What?!* you might say. *I thought I was being honest with God so that I'd feel better, not keep hurting.* David's prayer reminds us that God wants to reveal to us not only our sin but also the pain behind it. He has forgiveness *and* healing to offer to his children who are sinners *and* sufferers.

God isn't inviting you only to be honest about your sin; he truly desires to be your stronghold amidst the deepest pain and stress in your life. Why? He's our true Refuge and can take anything you bring to him and remake your heart's patterns into something new. This starts with being completely honest as David was.

Reflect: The Good Shepherd resists our resistance, chasing us down with his loving presence (see Ps. 23:6). Will you give up your "I can handle this myself" attitude? Will you accept God's request to come to him, pour out your heart, and listen for his merciful love, wise counsel, and tender comfort, which he knows you need?

Reflect: Like a surgeon's knife, which wounds to bring healing, the Holy Spirit uses the Word of God to cut through our self-deception and fear. The pain from God's soul surgery can be excruciating, but it's a part of the healing process! Trust your Soul Surgeon; he knows what he's doing. He makes no random cuts.

DAY 14

Admit Your True Fears

With my voice I cry out to the Lord; with my voice I
plead for mercy to the Lord. I pour out my complaint before him;
I tell my trouble before him. When my spirit faints within me, you know
my way! In the path where I walk they have hidden a trap for me.
Look to the right and see: there is none who takes notice of me;
no refuge remains to me; no one cares for my soul. (Ps. 142:1–4)

PEOPLE HAVE THE power to impact us in ways that plants, animals, entertainment, and the weather can't. We're image bearers with relational capacities that can be used to wound or to speak words of life (see Prov. 12:18), to shame or to offer love and comfort. These powers draw us toward one another and yet can also stir up fear and insecurity because we've all been disappointed—and worse—by other people.

David's cry to God from a cave reminds us that when we're fearful and troubled, we have godward steps we can take.

First, just like David cried out to the Lord, *we can put into honest words what we're scared about.* Naming our real fears before the Lord, wise friends, and ourselves can bring clarity about what's really driving our actions. For example, when they each got honest,

- Kari acknowledged that she was terrified of ongoing emotional discomfort in her marriage; Grace couldn't bear feelings of loneliness.
- Peter and Lynn feared what they would be left with if Emma wasn't in their daily lives. They were scared to really turn toward each other with their insecurities and longings.
- Sydney and Eric, though in very different circumstances, had a similar fear: they were afraid of being invisible, left

out, and unimportant; when these things happened, they felt intense pain.

- Michael consistently felt nervous that his internal messages were true: he wasn't worth anyone's love or respect, so it was on him to secure it.

Second, *we can hope!* David asked God to bring him out of his "prison" of fear when he was hunted and felt alone. By faith he knew that God could deliver him into a place of thankfulness. He had the audacity to believe that he could come out of his cave (literally and figuratively) into the presence of good people: "Bring me out of prison, that I may give thanks to your name! The righteous will surround me, for you will deal bountifully with me" (Ps. 142:7).

Third, *we can trust in the Lord.* Even if our circumstances don't change, we can trust in God who *will* deal bountifully with us. Because God has loved us through Christ (see Rom. 5:8), we don't have to be insecure or afraid or to feel ashamed of our fears.

Reflect: Can you identify the fears that motivate your relational patterns? Do you identify with one of the people above? Acknowledge this before the Lord and ask him to help you to trust that he is with you in your fears as your comforting, merciful Father.

Act: Perhaps you need to ask someone for help to get to the root of your fears. Who could you reach out to this week for prayer and encouragement? If no one comes to mind, ask God to help you to discover a journey companion who can help you.

DAY 15

Connect with Spiritual Family

But we were gentle among you, like a nursing mother taking care
of her own children. So, being affectionately desirous of you, we were
ready to share with you not only the gospel of God but also our own
selves, because you had become very dear to us. (1 Thess. 2:7–8)

PAUL HAD BEEN a violent antagonist to God's people (see Acts 9:1), yet he became a spiritual father like no other in the early church. He felt the tenderness of a nursing mother for the Thessalonian Christians and served them with the proactive discipleship of an engaged father (see 1 Thess. 2:6–12). Paul understood that the people of God are a spiritual family, eternal siblings bound together through the Father's adoption and the Elder Brother's sacrificial love.

Relationships within the body of Christ, through local churches, are crucial for our growth as followers of Jesus. God has no *only* children; you have many brothers and sisters, and it's important for you to proactively pursue relationships centered on the gospel through a community of faith.

Paul's words help us to understand a few ways that churches provide practical help for our growth in Christ, which includes relational maturity. First, they provide a local family where we are *known*. It may seem more convenient to stick to a me-and-Jesus approach, but God knows that we need outside help! Toxic relationships fester when we isolate ourselves from others. Or we refuse to let others into our lives because, like Michael in day 3, we think, "It's my business! Why should anyone else know?" Not surprisingly, Michael's marriage suffered for years because he was vague and avoidant whenever someone asked about it. He was ashamed of his struggles and scared to let anyone know about them.

Second, churches provide older brothers and sisters to *nurture and teach us.* Believers who are further down the road of spiritual maturity can know us specifically and then help us to discern what specific areas to focus on for growth. Identifying and smashing the idols in our lives, including those that lead to sin in our relationships, is tough work! God doesn't expect us to do this on our own. Paul models this both by the way he received help from believers and by the way he gave himself as a spiritual father and brother to so many.

Finally, Paul told the Thessalonians that they were "dear" to him. This affectionate word comes from one of the most powerful biblical words for love: *agape,* which means to love someone by "directing our will"[1] toward them with selfless care and service. Paul just mentioned how warmly desirous he was for them (see v. 8) and now assures them that not only does he have loving feelings toward them, he is lovingly committed to them. Christians are to love each other as Paul and Jesus modeled for us—by laying down our will for the benefit of others.

Wrapping these ideas together, we can see how local churches (when anchored in the truth, love, and grace of Jesus) provide a unique setting for us to be known, taught, and loved as we grow up in our faith. Growing up includes turning away from sin day after day, with spiritual friends and siblings to pray for us, encourage us, and challenge us to stay on the right path.

Reflect: If you don't have a church home, what steps can you take to find a local church that helps you to grow?

Act: It may seem scary to reach out to others, so consider praying something like "Father, help me to be willing to humbly ask other Christians for help. I can't do this on my own anymore and cry out to you to give me relationships like Paul had with the Thessalonians. Amen."

DAY 16

Renew Your Thinking about Relationships and Love

Do not be conformed to this world, but be transformed by the
renewal of your mind, that by testing you may discern what is the will
of God, what is good and acceptable and perfect. (Rom. 12:2)

THE HGTV NETWORK invites viewers to watch people discover their dream homes and to see houses be made radically new
through fresh design, color, furniture, and décor. In a similar way,
our thought lives need to be made completely new as Christ calls
us to die to self (completely bulldozing our former home of self)
and makes us a new creation with a new mind (see 1 Cor. 2:16;
2 Cor. 5:17). He actively changes us through his Spirit (see
Gal. 5:16–26) and commands us to engage the process of inner
renovation and transformation by renewing the way we think
about relationships and love.

Our verse today guides us in how to think holy, wise, pure,
and good thoughts (see Phil. 4:8–9). Paul teaches us to be holis-
tic in our faith, offering our entire life in service and worship to
the Lord (see Rom. 12:1). By renewing our minds in Scripture,
we can discern God's will and proactively resist worldly thinking.

How do we renew our minds? First, *we commit to reading*
and meditating on God's Word so that it has a home in us (see
Col. 3:16). We actively tear down thinking that is infested with
selfish motivations and false ideas (think of killing termites and
demolishing rotten wood, fake steel rods, and so on) and build
new thoughts through the living, active Word of God. We read
the Bible, think about it, pray it, study it with other believers,
and let it pierce our hearts. Slowly over time our thinking about

everything, including relationships and what love really means, will begin to change.

Second, *we resist and flee influences that corrupt our thought life.* We toss out anything that soils our minds with selfishness, lust, fear, anger, or unbelief; we cut off paths to ungodly supply sources that keep our sinful thoughts nourished. The more we're washed in the Word of God, the easier it becomes to recognize when pollution has entered in.

Sydney's transformation catapulted forward when she began to understand she was a beloved daughter of God. She realized she had been disrespected in the name of love and had selfishly used men to get what she craved. She began to have a biblical, rather than merely physical or emotional, understanding of sex; it really was a beautiful gift created by God for the loving, holy context of marriage. She realized how certain movies and music planted distorted ideas in her mind about sex and romance. She committed to stay away from entertainment that distracted her from Christ and asked a friend to ask her if she was faithfully sticking to her commitment.

Jesus loves us so much that he doesn't just tell us to do the right thing; he also helps us to think the right thoughts and to desire holiness. Through the Word made flesh and the transforming power of Scripture, your thought life can be completely remade, and so can your relationships.

Reflect: Are there influences in your life that pollute your thinking with selfish and/or sensual ideas regarding relationships?

Act: What steps do you need to take to have God's Word dwell in you more deeply (see Col. 3:16)?

DAY 17

Stop Living for People's Love and Love Them Instead

For the love of Christ controls us, because we have concluded this:
that one has died for all, therefore all have died; and he died for all,
that those who live might no longer live for themselves but for him
who for their sake died and was raised. (2 Cor. 5:14–15)

TODAY'S VERSES OFFER a counterintuitive yet transformational principle: wholeness in our relationships comes as we stop living for ourselves and instead start living for Christ. This contrast emerges in verse 15: "that those who live might no longer live for themselves *but for him.*" The "him" is Christ, "who for their sake died and was raised." The gospel tells us that God demonstrated his love by sending Christ for our sake so we no longer live dominated by our selfish, self-oriented ways but instead give ourselves wholeheartedly to Christ. And when we do, Jesus's love controls everything we do.

The next step is surprising—God first reconciles us to himself through Christ, then makes us "new creations" that turn outward to show Christ's love to others. Here's the second counterintuitive yet transformational principle: wholeness in our relationships grows as we root ourselves in Christ's love, stop living for people's love, and instead love others.

Paul calls us, controlled by Christ's love, to live as ambassadors of God's message of reconciliation (see 2 Cor. 5:18–20). To be his ambassadors means that we don't live for ourselves anymore but for our King and his glory. We represent him to the world around us, including the relational spheres where he has placed us. His values, methods, purposes, and message can be known and "fragrant" (see 2 Cor. 2:14) through us as we daily die to self and live for him.

Praying 2 Corinthians 5:14–15 has been significant for my relationships. One friendship consistently felt disappointing because, try as I might, I just couldn't achieve my secret inner goal to be needed and made much of. Another friend had the audacity to develop a close relationship with someone else! In these situations, God reminded me: *Ellen, you don't belong to yourself; you're Christ's, and he wants his love to compel you outward in loving people rather than demanding they love you on your terms.*

Jesus calls us to a lifestyle of loving obedience, and that includes engaging in his ambassadorial mission to this world. When I place my security in Christ alone, I find that my heart is stirred to serve others. Insecurity turns us inward; security in Christ sends us outward to bless, encourage, comfort, and assist others regardless of how they return the favor. The more we are controlled by Christ's love, the more we are freed up to do the good works he has prepared for each of us to walk in (see Eph. 2:10).

Reflect: Scripture promises that all believers have spiritual gifts (see Rom. 12:6–8 and 1 Peter 4:10–12) so that the body of Christ will be built up and that the gospel will go out to the world. How has God gifted you to serve others rather than demand they serve you?

Act: Serving other people honors the Lord and helps us to grow into Christlikeness. How can you love someone this week with the gifts he's given to you?

DAY 18

Live Hidden in Plain Sight

*But thanks be to God, who in Christ always leads us in
triumphal procession, and through us spreads the fragrance
of the knowledge of him everywhere. (2 Cor. 2:14)*

For you have died, and your life is hidden with Christ in God. (Col. 3:3)

COLOSSIANS 3:3 REVEALS in one sentence a mysterious
aspect of the gospel: that our true self is hidden with Christ, who
is our life (see Col. 3:4). The spiritual union we now share with
Christ because he dwells in our hearts can't be posted on social
media or seen or heard. However, our hiddenness is meant to
manifest in visible, tangible ways as God makes his "fragrance"
known everywhere through us!

When we disregard our oneness with Jesus, forgetting our
true identity as dead to self yet gloriously alive in him, we can
be tempted to seek to achieve elsewhere what can only come
from being united to and hidden in him. We turn to a person and
work hard to be perfectly seen, known, loved, pursued, valued,
complete, secure, and satisfied. Connections with people that
depend on experiencing affirmation, attention, and control are
in part the result of our refusal to live hidden in Jesus. We work
feverishly to not be forgotten by, abandoned by, or unimportant
to someone else.

Our verses today help to free us up to enjoy people with
healthy love. Paul can't help thanking God because he knows
that he and Jesus are joined together. Paul knows that because of
Christ within him, he's safe, loved, and at home. He goes where
Jesus goes, and Jesus goes with him! He participates in resurrection life and in the Jesus-exalting procession that spreads the

fragrance of Christ. Paul doesn't crave to be at the head of the parade, and he's not insisting to be the one waving to the crowd, drawing attention to himself. No, he knows he is hidden in Jesus, sharing life with his risen Lord *for the Lord* (see Eph. 5:1–2).

For years, Peter and Lynn thought they were selfless parents. Counsel from their pastor helped them to realize they had turned their *desires* for appreciation and closeness with Emma into a *demand* for those things. They had worked hard to be seen and heard by their daughter and hadn't understood how to bring Jesus into their relationship with her. Slowly they took steps to die daily to their demand that she need them; they studied what it meant to live "in Christ" rather than "in Emma's fixed attention" upon them. Lynn grieved the loss of daily contact with her daughter, and Peter battled feelings of insecurity as a father and husband. They were honest with God and each other, admitted their fears, and leaned into God as their Refuge. They took steps to live by dying daily, which allowed the fragrance of Christ's life to become more prominent in their relationship with Emma. Time with her became a gift to enjoy, rather than the result of their manipulation. Their motivation for involvement in her life changed from their need to be needed into an increasing thankfulness to love and serve her. In the wondrous counterintuitive power of the gospel, their daily dying produced life and joy, which helped Emma to feel safe, rather than imprisoned, through her parents' initiation.

Reflect: If you recognize in yourself a demand to be seen, praised, or needed by others, how can our verses today reorient your priorities and desires?

Act: Read Colossians 3:3 in the context of verses 1–4, and meditate on its promises and commands.

DAY 19

Practice Joy, Prayer, and Thankfulness

Rejoice always, pray without ceasing, give thanks in all circumstances;
for this is the will of God in Christ Jesus for you. (1 Thess. 5:16–18)

WHEN WE DEPEND on a person to make us happy or insist on being someone's mini-messiah, we'll live opposite of today's verses. Rather than *experiencing joy*, we turn in on ourselves with anxiety or turn out against others with jealousy and complaints. *Pray constantly?!* We don't have time or mental or emotional energy. Rather than *having thankful hearts*, we're discontent, never able to be satisfied with what people are offering us; it's never enough, and we deserve more, *right*?!

Ouch. I know, I've lived in that paragraph far too often, wasting opportunities that were meant to propel me toward God for help and to selflessly love others. If you're there today, here's what you can do. Take a step in the direction of three daily practices, which we know God will use to help us because they are his will for us in Christ. These seemingly simple steps can transform the way you view relationships because they place your focus on Christ.

Rejoice. Paul isn't saying that we make light of heartache and disappointment. This isn't a command to fake happiness. Joy is a fruit of the Holy Spirit within you. You can't produce it on your own, but the One in whom you are hidden can! The command to rejoice directs you to trust in the Lord's faithfulness to his Word and to you.

Pray without ceasing. Because we live in constant union with the Lord, we can have unbroken fellowship with him. Our experience of this isn't perfect while we live on earth because we get distracted, lazy, unmotivated, and more. God commands us to live in dependent humility upon him. When we develop a heart posture of trust and of dependent humility upon God, we talk to him about troubling relationships, painful disappointment, discontentment, and so on rather than musing on them in our own heads.

Give thanks in everything. When we demand that people be our gods, we are robbed of joy, heartfelt prayer, and thankfulness because our focus is no longer on Christ. A lifestyle of gratitude is possible only through faith in Jesus alone. The more we know Christ personally and deeply through the Scriptures, the more we will trust and rest in him. We thank him for who he is; we thank him for what he does; and we thank him that we belong to him. These three things alone will give you plenty to be thankful about!

Elizabeth, an older woman with a miraculous baby in her womb, beautifully models rejoicing, prayer, and selfless thankfulness. When Mary arrives to share news of her miraculous child, Elizabeth responds with humility and joy instead of making the occasion all about herself. She humbly acknowledges that her baby leaped for joy because of Mary's! She gladly blesses Mary with words of love and affirmation and praises the coming of the Lord (see Luke 1:39–45). Elizabeth wasn't perfect, but she was joyful and thankful. Her joy and gratitude freed her to love Mary with no strings attached, with no demands. Now that is fragrant love!

Reflect: When you ponder these three daily practices, which one seems to need the most attention from you right now? Ask God to help you to take steps in that direction.

Act: Even if you're currently facing disappointment with someone, what *can* you give thanks for? Push through your feelings and offer sacrificial thanksgiving to God!

DAY 20

Set Your Heart on Heaven

*Let us run with endurance the race that is set before us, looking to
Jesus, the founder and perfecter of our faith, who for the joy that
was set before him endured the cross, despising the shame, and is
seated at the right hand of the throne of God. (Heb. 12:1–2)*

RECENTLY, ONE OF my pastors breathed his last earthly
breath—in the next moment he was in the presence of Christ in
heaven! His memorial service was filled with honest grief, moving worship songs of faith, and words of thankfulness for a man
who had lived and had died *well*. A friend commented how just
a year earlier, before his diagnosis, our pastor had said that when
he died he wanted the love and presence of Christ in his life to
be what people remembered, not a list of ministry accomplishments. He was committed to running his faith race by living backward—in other words, by focusing on the life to come and letting
that impact the way he approached current trials and blessings,
his ministry, and a world of relationships.

Imagine that your life has ended and you are face-to-face with
Christ. Your earthly days are done, and you are living where tears,
disappointment, and interpersonal pain are no more. Relationships that once fueled jealousy, disappointment, or codependency are redeemed and made beautiful. Your sin and the mess
created by your selfish choices are done and gone.

To set our hearts on heaven, we must live now in light of
where we are ultimately going. The writer to the Hebrews teaches
us how—by "looking to" (or being fixed on) Jesus (Heb. 12:1),
who is enthroned in heaven (see Col. 3:1–3). This biblical truth
has helped me so much in my relational struggles. When jealousy and insecurity have hijacked my heart, I remember that

the circumstances that triggered these feelings will soon be done. When I've been displaced in someone's life and grieve the changed relational terrain, my faith is lifted up by locating Jesus again, gazing upon him as my destination and home.

To live *now* with peace and contentment, as we are "grieved by various trials" (1 Peter 1:6), it's important to remember where we are going. In heaven we will be fully enveloped in the glory of the Lord, worshipping Christ and astounded by his beauty, holiness, and love. We won't be fearful of missing out or enslaved to people's attention, because we will be fully satisfied with God. Any shame and embarrassment we've carried will be forgotten because we'll be face-to-face with Jesus.

Grab the end of the story when your race is done—no more relational idolatry; worshipping Christ for eternity—and insert this ending into your life right now. Our goal is to stay faithful to Christ, with a growing trajectory of trust in our true Refuge, King, and Satisfaction. You're not alone, and it won't be long before you're with Jesus!

Act: Richard Baxter, a Puritan pastor from the 1600s, encouraged people to take thirty minutes a day to meditate on heaven. Can you take a few minutes right now to mediate on heaven?

Act: If you know your heart's focus is rarely on the hope of heaven, consider praying something like "Lord, I confess that I think so much more about this life and what I see, feel, and hear. Help me to fix my eyes on Jesus and warm my heart with love for him. Give me a desire to be sober minded and alert to the enemy's schemes to hijack my focus off of you and onto this life. Most of all, Lord, deepen my understanding of what it means to set my hope fully on you. Amen."

Anchor Your Hope in Jesus

*According to [God's] great mercy, he has caused us to be born
again to a living hope through the resurrection of Jesus Christ from the
dead, to an inheritance that is imperishable, undefiled, and unfading,
kept in heaven for you. . . . Therefore, preparing your minds for action, and
being sober-minded, set your hope fully on the grace that will be brought
to you at the revelation of Jesus Christ. (1 Peter 1:3–4, 13)*

We have this as a sure and steadfast anchor of the soul. (Heb. 6:19)

THROUGHOUT THIS DEVOTIONAL, we have seen how our
hope is misplaced when we look to a person to satisfy all our emotional desires and needs. Our verses today anchor us in the truth
that we need to hold fast to our true hope through Jesus.

Peter begins his letter, which is written to suffering Christians,
by praising God for his active compassion toward those enduring
the misery of a sinful world. God's mercy through Jesus assures
us of spiritual life today that will never die out and of the fact that
in the not too distant future, we'll experience this spiritual life as
beautifully untarnished.

Friend, you have a living hope through your relationship
with Jesus, and God has promised you that in Christ you have an
eternal refuge of never-diminishing love—a living hope that can
transform your life, relationships, and suffering today! If you want
to grow in being hope*full*, fill your mind with truth about Jesus,
seeking to understand what is yours in him, both now and forever.
Speak to yourself, rehearsing the soul-steadying, hope-filled realities about God the Creator as your Refuge, Home, and Spouse
forevermore.

Peter's words in verse 13 echo what the writer to the Hebrews
said yesterday. Set your heart's gaze and hope fully on Jesus and

what is to come rather than this life and the gifts you enjoy through God's mercy. When we seek our living hope in an earthly relationship, we unanchor ourselves from Christ's promises, setting ourselves adrift in an unpredictable sea. A person's love, words of affection, need, and praise of us can never be "imperishable, undefiled, and unfading"; they don't have the power! We undo unhealthy hope we've placed on people by honestly expressing to God our pain, sin, and fears; renewing our thinking; practicing prayerful thankfulness; living through Christ's life and love; and walking alongside other believers with our focus on Jesus.

You have a living hope, and his name is Jesus. His love is an anchor, firm and secure for you amid the miserable tossing of sin and the suffering that has crashed over you. You have a future hope, a home that God is guarding as he longingly waits for you. You will get there sooner or later, so take a step today to relocate your hope upon the grace, love, and peace of Jesus our Lord.

Reflect: Review day 20 and consider how setting your heart on Christ in heaven, your ultimate destination and home, can fuel hope that helps you today.

Act: Our next section is focused on getting to know Jesus better! Scan the titles for days 22–31 and pray that your love for and dependence on Jesus will grow as you get to know more about him.

JESUS IS THE LOVING REFUGE WHO PROVIDES ALL YOU NEED

If I find in myself a desire which no experience in this world can satisfy, the most probable explanation is that I was made for another world. If none of my earthly pleasures satisfy it, that does not prove that the universe is a fraud. Probably earthly pleasures were never meant to satisfy it, but only to arouse it, to suggest the real thing. If that is so, I must take care, on the one hand, never to despise, or to be unthankful for, these earthly blessings, and on the other, never to mistake them for the something else of which they are only a kind of copy, or echo, or mirage. I must keep alive in myself the desire for my true country, which I shall not find till after death; I must never let it get snowed under or turned aside; I must make it the main object of life to press on to that country and to help others to do the same.

C. S. Lewis, *Mere Christianity*

DAY 22

Jesus Is a Refuge We Can Trust

"Let not your hearts be troubled. Believe in God; believe also in me.
In my Father's house are many rooms. If it were not so, would I have told
you that I go to prepare a place for you? . . . I will come again and will take
you to myself, that where I am you may be also." (John 14:1–3)

IN THE LAST hours before Jesus was arrested, he gave his friends several commands and promises. He wanted his friends to trust that he could be counted on to do what he promised; he wouldn't leave them like abandoned children because they were eternally secure as sons of his Father. Jesus was their Refuge and would always be someone they could turn to and trust.

Remember Kari and Grace, who we first met in day 6? After a year of their emotionally entangled and consuming friendship, Grace broke. The Holy Spirit used the inner turmoil of their messy dependency, coupled with a painful confrontation by Kari's husband, to convict her. Grace had to face it: instead of anchoring her hope in Jesus, she had done the opposite by working hard to soothe her troubled heart through Kari's affection. Her craving to have Kari be her emotional home through obsessive contact hadn't resulted in a satisfying, peace-filled, loving friendship; these women had a jealousy-filled prison that was threatened by anyone who tried to get in.

Grace felt heartbroken and miserable, but she turned to the Lord with her weak faith. She honestly cried to him, "Lord, I'm in so much pain, and I'm scared. Life without Kari?! Help me to trust you with what's on the other side of letting go of this relationship. . . . I'm afraid of facing the black hole in my heart." Her raw transparency with Christ emboldened her to confide in a wise older woman at her church and to share the real deal of her situation. She chose to believe the Lord and his Word more than what she *felt* in those early days after she told Kari she needed an extended break from being in contact. Over time, her tears of pain transformed to tears of joy at finally feeling free again as she took refuge in her trustworthy Lord.

When we're in stormy circumstances, sometimes the last thing we think is "God, what are you calling me to do right now?" Obedience to God grows our trust in Christ even when our emotions are rattled. His trustworthy promises give us hope!

I'll always tell you what you need to know.

I'm preparing a place for you in my Father's house. . . . I'm going to come back for you.

We'll always be in this together . . . believe me, trust me.

When you feel vulnerable, scared, and out of your comfort zone, turn to Jesus in prayer. If what you've read in this devotional has convinced you to take some scary steps of faith, tell Jesus how you feel! If you're unsure of where obedience is going to take you, ask Jesus to calm your fears and deepen your assurance that he is with you. Trustworthy and gentle-hearted, he knows how to lead you forward in the next step toward relational health.

Reflect: Which of Jesus's promises to you are most meaningful? Why?

Act: What steps of faith do you sense God calling you to take in regard to any specific relationships? Ask God to show you how to take the first step of obedience, and trust that he is aware of what's on the other side of that step!

DAY 23

Jesus Is Our Constant Companion

Christ in you, the hope of glory. (Col. 1:27)

For you have died, and your life is hidden with Christ in God. (Col. 3:3)

YEARS AGO I traveled from Romania to Austria to visit my brother. One day I explored Vienna alone and enjoyed beautiful parks, architecture, and cafes. More than twenty-five years later, I can vaguely remember sitting alone on a bench, taking in the splendor of an exquisite park on a sunny day. However, I have a strong memory of how struck I was by this thought as I sat there: "No one knows where I am but you, Lord!" In that moment, a combination of loneliness and comfort came over me. Humanly speaking, I was alone, yet I profoundly experienced God's presence as I sat on that bench. Jesus was with me. This became a pivotal spiritual truth for me.

Our spiritual DNA bears witness that we are created to be known, loved, and companioned. Desires for these good gifts reflect our relational God. Sometimes unhealthy attachments to people develop when we let fear of being alone and unknown control us. Our emotions can convince us we'll be swallowed up by a black pit of pain if we don't have a best friend, a perfect spouse, or a mentor who is our 24-7 source of encouragement and comfort.

When we seek a never-failing, constant connection with someone, we are setting ourselves up for disappointment at best and a broken relationship at worst. Disappointment because no person can bear the full weight of another's emotional needs. A broken relationship because it's exhausting and disillusioning to attempt a merging of lives that displaces God with another—sooner or later someone changes, moves on, or dies.

Most of us avoid goodbyes—they're usually painful, awkward, or emotionally scary. When Jesus said goodbye to his followers, he promised his constant presence—and not from a distant throne or celestial palace. No! He said, "And behold, I am with you always, to the end of the age" (Matt. 28:20). Through Christ living within us by the Spirit, God alone is our constant companion—we are hidden in him as he is mysteriously in us.

The truth that Jesus is with us is what Paul is getting at in our readings today: we are *in* Christ as he is *in* us. People may go away, relationships may dissolve, love may grow stale, but God's love and presence through Jesus are sure, steady, and constant, whether we feel them or not. These truths give us great hope when fixing an entangled relationship seems impossible and great comfort when someone we've clung to for life demands to be set free.

Jesus will never entangle himself with us or imprison us with selfish demands—with gracious love, our constant companion sets us free from the inside out.

Reflect: Does someone seem to want you to hide yourself in him or her, to merge your life with his or hers? Are you striving for someone to be your ultimate refuge? What difference could it make to really believe that you are hidden in and belong to Jesus?

Act: This week, go somewhere alone, even if only for thirty minutes, where no one but God knows exactly where you are. Tell him how you feel, what you're scared of, and how you need help believing and resting in his presence.

DAY 24

Jesus Is Our Redeemer Who *Is* the Good News

*"The Spirit of the LORD is upon Me, because He has anointed
Me to preach the gospel to the poor; He has sent Me to heal the
brokenhearted, to proclaim liberty to the captives and recovery of sight
to the blind, to set at liberty those who are oppressed; to proclaim the
acceptable year of the LORD." Then [Jesus] closed the book, and gave
it back to the attendant and sat down. And the eyes of all who were
in the synagogue were fixed on Him. (Luke 4:18–20 NKJV)*

DID YOU CATCH what happened in this scene?! As Jesus reads
the description of the promised Messiah, the audience hears this
humble man say, *I'm here; I'm the one! What you've heard from the
scrolls of Isaiah written in the past has now become present tense in
your presence.*

Christ is the author, bearer, and fulfillment of the good news
of the gospel. Christianity is anchored not only in the fulfillment
of an ancient promise but in a real person who embodies God's
Word. The words of Isaiah have been realized through the living
and active ministry of Jesus to

- transform our spiritual state as poor, lost, alienated, hopeless captives into freed sons and daughters;
- heal our broken hearts;
- give us spiritual sight and wisdom so we can supernaturally
  see Christ for who he is (in part now, but one day fully);
- carry our burdens and protect us from the crushing of this
  broken world, even as trials crash over us;
- proclaim freedom, safety, and rescue over us as we are
  raised up through the resurrection.

Our Redeemer has come! Are your eyes fixed upon him? Toxic relationships consume our attention and enslave us; Jesus sets us free as we obey him. Emotional enmeshments with people blind us to what is true and healthy; Jesus gives us sight to see ourselves and people rightly. When we cling to a person and demand that he or she be our savior, we will be disappointed; only Jesus is faithful and trustworthy.

Michael and Jackie (from day 3) needed marriage help. After years of Jackie's persevering love, Michael finally reached out to a Christian brother for help and began to face the insecurity and anger that fueled his selfish demands on his wife. Over time and honest conversation, he began to recognize how he had fixed his hope on Jackie, not Jesus. He had unknowingly believed the lie that she could (and should!) heal his heart and set him free from insecurity. As Michael grew to direct his spiritual eyes toward Jesus, he was amazed at how much he began to enjoy Jackie—discontent was replaced with thankfulness, and humility defused his anger. Confidence grew as Michael began to identify more with Jesus and shifted his focus away from striving to get from Jackie what could be found only in his Redeemer.

Jesus is your Redeemer. He is the good news you need and the one God created your heart to desire the most. He was anointed and sent to proclaim *and be* the news we all need. Jesus accomplishes God's mission to rescue needy sinners and sufferers, like you and me. Gently and faithfully, he can adjust the gaze of your heart and needs. Will you fix your eyes on him?

Act: What insecurities and fears distract you from Jesus? Who or what is drawing your gaze elsewhere? Confess this to the Lord and ask for help to fix your eyes on Christ.

Reflect: Look again at today's text and consider all the reasons that Jesus came. Which of our Redeemer's ministries most connect with your heart today?

DAY 25

Jesus Sees Us at Every Moment

*And [Zacchaeus] was seeking to see who Jesus was, but on account of
the crowd he could not, because he was small in stature.... And when
Jesus came to the place, he looked up and said to him, "Zacchaeus, hurry
and come down, for I must stay at your house today." (Luke 19:3, 5)*

*Nathanael said to him, "How do you know me?"
Jesus answered him, "Before Philip called you, when you
were under the fig tree, I saw you." (John 1:48)*

A CLOSE FRIEND and I often say to each other, "I see you.
... I'm with you!" even though we live on opposite sides of the
United States. Years of sharing our hearts and lives with each
other have enabled us to know each other deeply so we're able to
empathize with each other's joys and struggles, even though time
spent face-to-face is infrequent.

My friend and I, however, have misread each other many
times. No person has the ability to see, know, and understand
us perfectly. Have you ever felt invisible in social situations? You
know, at the party, or women's Bible study, or exercise class when
you come alone and no one greets you. At the men's retreat, when
most are out having recreation time, and you just don't feel like
you belong. At the weekly meeting on campus where you feel like
you're the only introvert in a loud, smiley-faced crowd of people
who appear cool and fun.

Zacchaeus and Nathanael had a lot in common. They were
both Israelites, curious about Jesus, and the recipients of his
focused, purposeful gaze. Jesus's words to them communicated,
*Zacchaeus, Nathanael, I have always seen you and I see you now; I
love you and want a relationship with you.*

Healthy relationships develop when we rest in the gaze of

Jesus. The loving look of Jesus upon us 24-7 comforts us when someone misses us completely or ignores us in detached, selfish preoccupation. No matter how hard we try to get the attention of others, no one can *see* us the way he does!

How did Zacchaeus feel when Jesus not only saw him but honored him before a crowd? What was it like for Nathanael to hear that Jesus's gaze had always been on him, even though they had just met face-to-face?

You might believe you are "small in stature" like Zacchaeus, feeling different from others because of your appearance, abilities, or weaknesses. Maybe you resonate with Nathanael, a man with significant spiritual blind spots who was nonetheless commended by Jesus.

Jesus is with us always and sees and understands our hearts. Your dearest relationship can offer you tastes of how Jesus sees and moves toward us, lifts us up, and invites us to draw near. Yet he alone *sees* and knows us perfectly, including our blind spots and weaknesses, and commends us as children of God with hope and grace. This, my friend, is the kind of *seeing* we need the most when insecurity, jealousy, or loneliness blinds us to God's mercy and care!

Reflect: What tends to be your reaction when you feel invisible to someone, especially a person whose attention you crave? How are you encouraged by Jesus's response to Zacchaeus and Nathanael?

Act: When we feel invisible and unwanted, usually the last thing we want to do is reach out to love someone else. Is there someone in your life whom you can seek to *see* and move toward this week, rather than working at being noticed yourself? *Seeing* is a way to love others!

DAY 26

Jesus Mercifully Listens to Us

*And he said, "Jesus, remember me when you come into your
kingdom." And he said to him, "Truly, I say to you, today
you will be with me in paradise." (Luke 23:42–43)*

SHE CAUGHT ME. A close friend called me out when in the
middle of a face-to-face conversation, I was distracted by a notifi-
cation that popped up on the screen of my smartphone. In a second, I exited my real-time conversation with her and turned to
my phone. Effectively, I turned away from my friend, closing my
ears to her, and listened to the voice of my phone.

Ugh. I've selfishly done this to people more often than I want
to admit. I've also been the recipient of distracted listening and
know how it feels. *What?! I'm not as important as your device's
notifications? What's so interesting out the window that you can't stay
focused on our conversation?*

Listening without distraction is a powerful way to love someone. Jesus's brief conversation with the criminal on the cross
elevates the power of loving listening. As he hung on the cross,
bloodied and separated from God, Jesus showed mercy to a hurting sinner. He listened attentively to this man's request, offered
words that proved he was listening well, and gave a dying man the
hope of eternal companionship with God.

Consider the risk taken by this bold criminal hanging on his
deserved cross next to the sinless Savior. Would Jesus ignore him?
Would the Savior, who had every reason to reject him, hear what
he had to say? This sinful man had every reason to stay silent during his last hours of life. He heard the crowd's mocking and the
shameful things that others said to Jesus, yet the criminal spoke
up to defend Jesus and then boldly spoke to the despised One.

This criminal evidently knew what Jesus had taught about being the fulfillment of Scripture's prophecy of the holy Messiah and courageously asked to be remembered by him in his kingdom.

Jesus listens, responds, and makes a promise to this criminal, transforming him into a humble disciple. Amazing grace goes from Savior to sinner, the fruit of attentive mercy. The voice of God drowns out the voice of sinful choices, shaming antagonists and alleviating incredible fear as the criminal faces death. The Savior of the world listens to, forgives, and saves the suffering sinner hanging next to him.

Jesus sees you and listens to the cries of your heart, whether they arise from a self-centered place or a sincere desire for help. What do you want to say to him now? Jesus, the criminal's Savior and yours, has words of love and hope for you. He mercifully listens to your words, cries, and needs.

Reflect: Whose listening ear do you want the most, and why? What is it about that person's attention to and knowledge of you that is so important?

Reflect: Idolatrous relationships distract us not only from talking to the Lord but also from listening to him! Rather than turning toward Jesus, we turn toward a friend, child, spouse, or mentor, desperate to hear a word of affirmation or affection that assures us we are the center of that person's focus, need, or gaze. When we seek the love of people more than the loving truth of God, we're swayed; we eventually sink into fear and discontent.

DAY 27

Jesus Speaks to Our
Father about Us

He is able to save to the uttermost those who draw near to God through him, since he always lives to make intercession for them. (Heb. 7:25)

PRAYER IS AN intimate invitation into relationship with God; he loves us and wants to hear our fears, joys, concerns, and problems firsthand. But we don't pray alone or in our own power. Jesus and the Spirit not only *help* us to pray but actually pray *for* us.

Today's verse says Jesus always prays for those whom he has saved. As he sits at the right hand of the Father, he is interceding for us (see Rom. 8:34). That means if you are wrestling with insecurity, stuck in a hard relational moment, or scared of another's opinion and don't know what to pray, don't panic. If you don't have the words to speak or you're struggling to pray, take comfort. Jesus is already talking to our Father on your behalf. Supernaturally, he takes our unarticulated pain and confusion that we just can't put into words and expresses it to our Father with perfect understanding.

Jesus is interceding for you right now from the right hand of God, and you can be sure that if a toxic relationship is distracting, even destroying you, this is a topic on his heart! The anguish and fear usually connected to repenting from relational idolatry can suffocate our prayers, but Jesus and the Holy Spirit are never hindered in their prayerful "groanings" for you (Rom. 8:26–27). Right now, as you read today's devotional, Jesus and the Holy Spirit are asking the Father to move powerfully on your behalf. As our constant and indwelling friend, Jesus takes our needs and concerns to the Father who hears and responds.

Remember also that Jesus taught his followers to pray as a family, "*Our* Father in heaven" (Matt. 6:9), not "*My* Father in heaven." This is so important for us to remember because while our relationship with Jesus *is* personal to each of us, we are never separated from the body of Christ, our brothers and sisters who call on the same Father. As we discussed on day 15, you have spiritual family who can pray with and for you!

Reflect: How does it help you to consider that Jesus and the Holy Spirit are interceding for you, always in unity with the will of the Father? How does this help you to let go of any internal pressure to pray "correctly" or eloquently?

Act: If you are struggling to pray, start with short, simple prayers: "Lord, help me today," or "Lord, I need your comfort," or "Jesus, help me to believe that you are trustworthy and powerful to change me." Take a verse or passage from Scripture and pray it to God as a personal cry for help: "Lord, help! Restore joy to my heart because of my salvation in Jesus . . . strengthen me to believe and obey you. And Lord, satisfy me with your love today and free me from demanding that [this person] meet all my needs" (see Ps. 51:12; 143:8). Don't make it complicated, but take a step toward the Lord by talking to him and sharing the honest feelings and thoughts that are troubling you. He *wants* to listen to you and does so with love.

Jesus Is Our Friend and Our Home

"If anyone loves me, he will keep my word, and my Father will love him, and we will come to him and make our home with him." (John 14:23)

"I have called you friends, for all that I have heard from my Father I have made known to you." (John 15:15)

IN THE FINAL hours before his death, Jesus taught his disciples important truths he knew they needed. In John 13–17, we hear our Savior's heart as he describes his upcoming death, departure from this world, and sending of the Spirit and tells his disciples how to do life, relationships, and ministry. In the middle of this time of discipleship with his friends, Jesus makes a promise about a radically new type of closeness between God and his people: being *at home* with each other.

At home with God? Jesus had just explained that the sending of the Holy Spirit would allow Christ to "come" to his followers (see John 14:15–18). He was preparing them for the miracle of the new covenant: spiritual intimacy through union between God and his people.

Union with Christ is the spiritual reality that Jesus is in us and we are in him. Messy relationships with people are transformed as we rest in the realities of our eternal intimacy with God. We have seen that in God through Christ we have a trustworthy Lord, Refuge, Spouse, Rescuer, and Counselor. Friend, in Christ we also have our truest, eternal home! He calls us "friends," "family," and the ones with whom he wants to be united forever.

Codependent relationships grow through unholy desires and expectations that a person be our ultimate home. The push-pull dance of enmeshed romantic relationships (dating or married) are fueled by a manipulative dynamic of each partner staying in his or her role as either the needy one or the rescuer-caregiver. Idolatrous friendships are fueled by an intoxicating belief that *we must guard our home in each other, our "us."* Parents like Peter and Lynn unknowingly cultivate an unhelpful (sometimes destructive) dependency upon themselves in their children by refusing to let their children become healthily independent. Their insecurity fuels unholy cleaving to children, hindering their ability to develop a life for themselves outside their literal and figurative home as a family.

Relationships can be a tremendous blessing, but even the healthiest and most intimate of marriages can only give a taste of our eternal, secure, unfailing love-filled home in Christ. The dearest kindred-hearted friendship is a gift meant to point beyond itself to the Friend who has made a home in us and who is himself our home, never to leave or replace us with someone else.

> **Act:** The idea of Jesus being your home may feel foreign at best, unappetizing at worst. You know he loves you, but you want to see a person and feel their arms holding you. People can feel warm and comforting; Jesus seems cold and distant. If you resonate with these thoughts, tell God and ask him to grow your understanding of the home we have in him.
>
> **Act:** Consider people in your life who seem secure in the Lord and relationally healthy. They enjoy and love people but aren't controlled by them. They are loving and kind, not manipulative or needy. Reach out to Christians like this and ask if they'd share with you how their relationship with God has helped them to develop meaningful, healthy relationships.

DAY 29

Jesus Considers Us His Family

Looking about at those who sat around him, [Jesus] said, "Here are my mother and my brothers! For whoever does the will of God, he is my brother and sister and mother." (Mark 3:34–35)

TODAY THE VALUE of family has diminished in the face of independence and autonomy, but within our hearts, there remains the desire for *home* and *belonging*. When you were younger, your home life may have been unstable or unsafe. Perhaps you felt you didn't belong. Unfortunately, broken families can inadvertently influence people to seek experiences of belonging, parenting, and nurture in destructive ways.

Jesus had an imperfect family too. They thought he was out of his mind (see John 7:5) due to the things he was teaching. Jesus didn't abandon his family of origin (see John 19:26–27), but he did consider those who do the will of God to be his true spiritual family. This public declaration was provocative in a culture that placed high value on honoring parents and loyalty to one's kindred.

Honestly facing disappointment with our family experiences can give insight into why we have sought to belong to or control someone to such a degree that we feel stuck in a prison of codependency. You play the role of mother in all your friendships. You're seeking spousal affection, like Grace, outside marriage, maybe from a friend, pastor, or counselor. Or like Eric, you're a ministry leader who's gotten off track and you use the pain and neediness of others to feel good about yourself. You're determined, like Michael, to make your spouse your savior.

Jesus's declaration about his true family can free us from these destructive patterns. Our Home and Friend offers the deep relationship you are truly seeking—that you deeply need! When he names us as his family, it's implied that we belong to him and have an inheritance that is ours through the gospel (see Gal. 4:4–7). When we keep these truths set firm in our beliefs, we can move through painful family experiences into healing that brings wholeness.

Has your heart been broken through a painful family experience? God your Father through Christ your elder brother will heal your heart! Do you feel desperate to belong to someone—or even to own someone—in an attempt to feel like you have meaning? Jesus, not a human relationship, will give you purpose and identity. Have you fearfully stayed in a toxic relationship because it's the only kind you know? Jesus will help you to walk away and find freedom—in the healthy Home of himself. Maybe you're isolated because attempting to grow healthy relationships is scary and daunting. The family of God through Christ is yours—to encourage and disciple you on how to form relationships based on holy, wise love.

"Whoever does the will of God, he is [my family]." Jesus had all believers in mind when he said this. You're not alone, and you never will be!

> **Reflect:** We can't blame our sinful choices on others, but we can gain insight by knowing how our history has influenced us. Can you identify ways your family experience has affected you—both helpfully and unhelpfully?
>
> **Act:** If you experienced trauma in your family or if certain painful experiences seem to exert persistent influence in your life now, consider reaching out to a spiritual leader or biblical counselor. This is yet another way that the family of God can help you!

DAY 30

Jesus Is Our Bridegroom

*"The one who has the bride is the bridegroom. The friend of the
bridegroom, who stands and hears him, rejoices greatly at the
bridegroom's voice. Therefore this joy of mine is now complete.
He must increase, but I must decrease." (John 3:29–30)*

WHEN I LIVED overseas as a single woman in a culture that
expected most to marry young, I received many questions. Once
I visited a family, and the father asked, "Ellen, isn't it difficult for
you to be alone? Don't you want to be married?" I don't remember my answer, but I recall my sadness at being seen as different
and unusual. However, a comforting thought came as I walked
home that day: "Lord, I'm walking alone here—at least that's
what they say and see—but what they don't see is that I'm with
you!" Though ringless, I had and have an eternal Bridegroom!

In today's verse, John the Baptist identifies Jesus as the long-
awaited Messiah, Bridegroom, and King whom the Old Testament promised. He knew that God had planned all along to relate
to his people as their Bridegroom (see Isa. 62:4–5). John will-
ingly stepped aside from the limelight with words that echoed
what Jesus, his Bridegroom, would say almost three years later:
"These things I have spoken to you, that my joy may be in you,
and that your joy may be full" (John 15:11).

The word translated as "complete" in John 3:29 and "full"
in John 15:11 means filled up or perfected. This filling, perfect
love is what Jesus our Bridegroom offers to his people, his bride.
His spousal love isn't like that of the most devoted wife or faithful husband; those human examples are *like him*. In fact, what
spouses can offer to each other is a reflection of the majestic love
that our King and Bridegroom Jesus shares with us, his people.

Has your marriage or hope for marriage become discon-nected from Jesus because human, romantic love seems more tangible and desirable? It's common for God's good gifts to loom larger than the Giver in our hearts. When this happens, our hope for joy and intimacy moves away from the Bridegroom and can lead to unrealistic expectations placed on people. Even friend-ships can take on a harmful "mini-marriage" feel as two people act like emotional spouses with each other. Jesus alone can bring fullness of joy into our hearts, which enables us to joyfully and healthily celebrate people and the love we share with them.

Does your heart need recalibration regarding your spiritual marriage and closeness with Jesus? He can help to get your joy back on track by anchoring it in his love for you. Not only is he a faithful Shepherd chasing us down with steadfast love (see Ps. 23:6), he is a passionate and protective Bridegroom, always ready to draw near to his bride!

Reflect: How do John's words strike your heart? Will you pray for deep joy in Jesus to grow in your heart?

Act: What would you like to say to the Lord in response to today's reading? Maybe a prayer like this will help you: "Lord Jesus, help me to understand how you are a Bridegroom to me and all of your people, the bride of Christ. Please grow in me the kind of faith and joy that John experienced, and cause it to impact the way I love people. Amen."

DAY 31

Jesus Invites Us to Join His Mission

For we are his workmanship, created in Christ Jesus for good works, which God prepared beforehand, that we should walk in them. (Eph. 2:10)

ONE OF THE ways we live out relational holiness is through participation in the kingdom work of King Jesus. Followers of Jesus throw off sinful entanglements and distractions *so that* we can run the race of faith unhindered (see Heb. 12:1–2). A life of healthy relationships is only part of the redemptive story—our Redeemer has a bigger, eternal picture in mind! Life becomes an adventure when we seek to discover what good works God has prepared specifically for us to live out.

Recently the truth of today's verse helped me as I yet again recognized relational idolatry rising up in my heart. As terrain in some relationships changed, I felt ignored, left behind, and insecure. The familiar pattern of response slowly rose up in my thoughts, tempting me to withdraw and succumb to anxiety. I allowed the focus of my desires and thoughts to be hijacked off Christ, resulting in jealousy, frustration and shame. *Really, I'm struggling with this again?!*

Then, the Savior who saves me from myself, our Father who comforts me in all my afflictions, and the wise Counselor who guides me back to what is true, intervened. I confessed my struggles to a few friends who loved me by listening and speaking truth to me about my emotions and thoughts. I remembered that Jesus runs my life, not me. He wanted me to join him on mission, to serve and encourage as this was why he had placed me in the situation in the first place. He was teaching me to rejoice with those who rejoice and to weep with those who weep (see Rom. 12:15). He allowed a story to unfold outside me so that I would know him as my constant companion who sees, listens, and responds to my cries for help. My true Home loved me back onto the path of faith and brought me peace through obedience that he enabled— new life came by dying to self.

Friend, there have been hard things to process in these thirty-one days. You have been called to die to self, to trust in God through surrender and obedience that often don't feel good. You've humbly allowed your world of relationships to be examined under the light of God's Word.

Now what? Jesus invites you not only to repent and be healed but to join him on mission! There are good works of Christ prepared for us as the family of God, and you have a unique part to play. Will you keep saying yes to Jesus, asking him to help you to grow into a lifestyle of holiness and wholeness in your relationships—to set your heart on things above, not on this earth? The Master of the mission is with you, and he will be faithful to complete the work he's started in you . . . one day at a time.

Reflect: Messy relationships often distract and rob us from good works that God wants us to participate in. Can you think of any ways you might engage the mission of Jesus in new ways over the next month?

Act: Take a moment to pray: "Father, Son, and Spirit, I honor you as my true Lord and Savior and the One in whom I live, move, and have my being. I praise you for the good work you've started and will faithfully complete in my life for your glory, and I ask that fullness of joy will be mine in Christ. Amen."

CONCLUSION

Continuing to Take Refuge in Christ

WHEN JESUS WINDS down what is known as the Sermon on the Mount, he shares a metaphor to guide us in building strong relationships.

> Everyone then who hears these words of mine and does them will be like a wise man who built his house on the rock. And the rain fell, and the floods came, and the winds blew and beat on that house, but it did not fall, because it had been founded on the rock. And everyone who hears these words of mine and does not do them will be like a foolish man who built his house on the sand. And the rain fell, and the floods came, and the winds blew and beat against that house, and it fell, and great was the fall of it. (Matt. 7:24–27)

Your life has the potential to be more *secure* and *peaceful* when you listen to Christ and act on what he says. You will be like the wise man who built his house (his life) upon the stable rock. The storms won't knock down the house because it's built on the rock, which is Christ himself. After thirty-one days of meditating on God's Word, are you willing to keep walking forward in your journey with Christ? To pray and seek him as your priority with the wisdom and commands of the Bible as the foundation of your life, including your relationships?

Christians live in constant, intimate relationship with the Rock himself. Jesus Christ has joined himself to us for eternity and instructs us to live in dependence upon him alone, obeying his commands and following his instructions for relationships. As we obey him, that leads to relationships in which we love people rather than use or fear people. It leads to courage and strength, even when the winds of conflict and disappointment beat upon us. We'll take steps of faith to let people off the hook and no longer demand that they be our savior. As we listen to Christ and do what he says, we'll experience more freedom and joy through our connections with people for what they are—a gift of God!

We've covered a lot of ground over these thirty-one days as we've thought about God, our sinful and hurting hearts, God's love and rescue of us, and practical steps to pursue growth. God wants to help you not only to experience wholeness and holiness in your relationships with people but to deepen your trust in him. Our Creator Lord really does want his people to celebrate life and the gift of relationships with others, to rejoice and delight in the "saints in the land" (Ps. 16:3) we encounter in this life!

So what do we do on day 32 and beyond? What's your next step of growth in your understanding of Jesus as your Rock, Refuge, Friend, Bridegroom, and Brother? Let's consider several things you might pray about and then seek to engage by faith and dependence upon God.

If you are in a relational mess and people idolatry is controlling your life, *find a mature Christian in your church, or talk with a spiritual leader you respect, and ask for help.* Proverbs 18:1 says, "Whoever isolates himself seeks his own desire; he breaks out against all sound judgment." You need to learn holy moderation and boundaries in your relationships, not bingeing or starving yourself. When we try to work out problems on our own in isolation, often we'll stay stuck. It's been said that the power of secret sin is in the secret. Don't tackle this alone!

Do you need to allow space between yourself and another person—or even end a relationship that is imprisoning you? If you answer yes to any of the following questions, this may be a step for you to take.

- Has a same-sex friendship become too physically affectionate and perhaps sexual?

- Are you dating someone who insists on controlling you, or whom you can't stop trying to control? Is one or both of you consistently jealous, threatened, or unhappy about other relationships in your life?
- Do you feel like you need to hide how much you're in contact with someone and the level of emotional intimacy you share? Why do you feel compelled to hide—what are you afraid of?
- Has a counseling, mentoring, discipling, or caregiving relationship taken over your life, as it did for Eric and Sydney? Has it crossed boundary lines of appropriate involvement?
- Family relationships (marriage, parent-child, siblings) need discernment about the process of stepping back, without stepping out of the relationship. While I've chosen to limit my application of the concept of toxic relationships, the sobering reality is that these kinds of connections can become abusive. Some people stay in abusive relationships due to many of the things we've discussed in this devotional. If this is an area of concern for you or someone you know, please consider reaching out to your pastor or another leader you trust. An excellent book I recommend is *Is It Abuse? A Biblical Guide to Identifying Domestic Abuse and Helping Victims* by Darby A. Strickland (P&R Publishing, 2020).

It may feel unloving and harsh to step away from someone or to end a relationship, but when your actions are motivated by obedience to God's Word, true love is at work! You can stand secure in Christ's promises today, knowing he will watch over the consequences of your obedience to him, including the impact it has on others. Ask someone to walk alongside you in regards to steps of repentance you need to take. *If you are not a member of a local, Jesus-loving, Bible-teaching, gospel-centered church, find one and join it.* There is no replacement for working these heart issues out in a loving, Christ-honoring gospel community—the spiritual family God has for you.

Consider rereading this devotional. Reading it a second time through allows you to personalize and internalize the content more deeply.

Stay in the Word. Don't settle for merely taking in the words of this devotional! Seek Christ and his Word, trusting that he will counsel and comfort you day after day. God's Word brings life to your soul. It points you daily to Christ. Meditate on it, and let the Word continue to reveal your heart idolatries and reorient you to Jesus.

Pray, pray, and then pray again. Your fellowship with God, your constant dependence on him, will grow as you pray. So pray without ceasing. Keep turning back to the Lord for help. Pray the Scriptures from each of the devotionals, perhaps choosing the passages that targeted your heart most specifically.

Keep the gospel in full view.[1] The more you let people rule your heart, the more insecure you will be. The more you ground yourself in the gospel, the more you'll have the potential of having happy and holy relationships, and the more sinful dynamics toward others will fade. Keep returning to the gospel in your reading, prayer, conversations—really, most everything you do.

Remember the marathon nature of the Christian life. We will spend our entire earthly lifetime being transformed into Christlikeness, so don't give up if unhealthy relational patterns seem to die a slow death. Our faith grows day by day as we walk forward toward Christ, and he will complete what he has started in you (see Phil. 1:6)!

Finally, *don't forget that your relational desires are meant to point you to Jesus!* The joy and love you can have with people truly are beautiful gifts, but they aren't the end goal. God alone is your Refuge as you take steps to grow into a relationally healthy person, battling temptations and sin in your relationships. We've seen that he, like a skillful surgeon, knows precisely where to cut into our hearts with his Word so as to create space for his truth, healing, and transformation. And we've been encouraged to understand how obedience involves practical, daily steps toward God and the truth of Scripture. We have a living, present, loving Lord, and he alone provides all we need in our lifelong walk of transformation and faith. Jesus Christ is God with us; he is and always will be our loving, trustworthy Refuge and Hope.

Acknowledgments

I'M THANKFUL TO my parents, Walter Sr. and Lucille Dykas, who taught me to depend on God in various ways. I can still remember Mom's words from decades ago when she gently corrected me with the words "God alone is to be adored," so that I would not put my hopes ultimately in people. She was a beautifully soft-spoken woman whose lived-out faith was loud with love.

My seven siblings and their families have loved and respected me in the life God has called me to. Thank you for cheering me on in my desire to be faithful to our true Refuge.

I'm grateful for several long-suffering, wise, and compassionate friends who have walked with me through some of my toughest battles with codependency and all the mess that goes with it. Thank you for loving me and encouraging me to delight in God's gift of people as an overflow of my relationship with him!

My staff family at Harvest USA has spurred me on, loved and prayed for me, and consistently pointed me toward Jesus Christ as my life, home, and eternal spouse. Truly, these brothers and sisters have companioned me for many years, helping me to grow not only as a woman in ministry but as a follower of Jesus.

Over many years of ministry, I've been entrusted with the struggles and stories of many people who have been mired down in toxic, codependent patterns. I'm grateful for how their humility and teachability were used to *teach me* so much about the things I've written in this devotional.

And Lord, what can I say, you truly are my life and love! Praise be to you, the one who has gone with me to every zip code and into every new situation and who has carried me out of so many situations. I delight to share life with you and to rest in your unfailing love. I desire to follow after you day after day . . . please help me to stay faithful to the finish line!

Notes

Introduction: Moving toward Your True Refuge

1. This will have a unique look for different relationships, and wisdom is especially needed in a marriage or in a parent-child relationship. See the list on pages 95–96 for additional resources that may help you.

Day 1: Our Refuge Now and Forever

1. See 2 Samuel 21–22 for the context of Psalm 18.

Day 2: Our Heart Healer

1. The word "brokenhearted" in Psalm 147:3 is the Hebrew word *shavar*. See definition in Spiros Zodhiates, ed., *The Complete Word Study Old Testament* (Chattanooga, TN: AMG Publishers, 1994), 2370.

Day 7: Our Eternal Source of Spousal Love

1. If you need help regarding sexual sin (personal or that of a family member), see Harvest USA's website, www.harvestusa.org.

Day 9: Suffering

1. Joseph Hart, "Come, Ye Sinners, Poor and Needy," 1759.

Day 15: Connect with Spiritual Family

1. The word "dear" in 1 Thessalonians 2:8 is *agapetos*, which comes from *agape*, meaning "to love," and "indicates a direction of the will and finding one's joy in something." Spiros Zodhiates, ed., *The Complete Word Study New Testament* (Chattanooga, TN: AMG Publishers, 1991), 878.

Conclusion: Continuing to Take Refuge in Christ

1. The gospel or good news of Jesus is mentioned all the time (rightly so!) among believers, yet sometimes the familiarity of a term can

rob us of a deeper understanding of a concept. The amazing story of God's gracious love through Jesus our Redeemer is the foundation of every page in this devotional. For a mercifully short book that can help you to understand the grace and depth of the gospel, see Greg Gilbert, *What Is the Gospel?* (Wheaton, IL: Crossway, 2010).

Suggested Resources for Your Encouragement

Brestin, Dee. *He Calls You Beautiful: Hearing the Voice of Jesus in the Song of Songs.* New York: Multnomah, 2017. [This book helps the reader to understand the Song of Songs as not only a picture of godly human love but also of Christ's love for his people.]

Miller, Paul E. *A Loving Life: In a World of Broken Relationships.* Wheaton, IL: Crossway, 2014. [Paul Miller unpacks the book of Ruth beautifully to help the reader to understand how the cross-centered life leads to radical love for people. I appreciate this book for the way it has discipled me to understand how to die to self so that the resurrection life of Christ be made known in my relationships.]

Needham, Kelly. *Friend-ish: Reclaiming Real Friendship in a Culture of Confusion.* Nashville: Nelson Books, 2019. [This is a wonderful book about godly, healthy friendship. Needham wisely unpacks what codependent/idolatrous dynamics look like in friendships, with applications that touch on other relationships as well.]

Packer, J. I. *Knowing God.* Downers Grove, IL: InterVarsity Press, 1973. [Packer's classic book lays a foundation for the development of healthy and holy relational patterns in our lives. When we understand who God is and who we are because of him, it transforms the way we view all of life, including our relationships.]

Silvious, Jan. *Please Don't Say You Need Me: Biblical Answers for Codependency.* Grand Rapids: Zondervan, 1989. [Jan's book came out long before other biblical writers were addressing codependency. A biblical counselor herself, she addresses toxic relational dynamics in friendship, marriage, and parent-child relationships.]

Smith, William P. *Loving Well: (Even if You Haven't Been).* Greensboro, NC: New Growth Press, 2012. [William (Bill) Smith mentored me while I was a biblical counseling student, so his words in this book have extra weight for me; I've seen the way he seeks to live out the contents of these pages. His words will point you to God's love as the only enabling power we have to trade bad relationship habits for Christ-centered security.]

Welch, Edward T. *When People Are Big and God Is Small: Overcoming Peer Pressure, Codependency, and the Fear of Man.* Phillipsburg, NJ: P&R Publishing, 1997. [Ed's book was my introduction to biblical counseling and helped me to take the first true gospel-centered steps of repentance from people idolatry. This book lays an excellent foundation with practical application for the various ways codependency can manifest, whether in marriage, parenting, friendships, work environments, and so on. The title says it all!]

BIBLICAL
COUNSELING
COALITION

The Biblical Counseling Coalition (BCC) is passionate about enhancing and advancing biblical counseling globally. We accomplish this through broadcasting, connecting, and collaborating.

Broadcasting promotes gospel-centered biblical counseling ministries and resources to bring hope and healing to hurting people around the world. We promote biblical counseling in a number of ways: through our *15:14* podcast, website (biblicalcounselingcoalition.org), partner ministry, conference attendance, and personal relationships.

Connecting biblical counselors and biblical counseling ministries is a central component of the BCC. The BCC was founded by leaders in the biblical counseling movement who saw the need for and the power behind building a strong global network of biblical counselors. We introduce individuals and ministries to one another to establish gospel-centered relationships.

Collaboration is the natural outgrowth of our connecting efforts. We truly believe that biblical counselors and ministries can accomplish more by working together. The BCC Confessional Statement, which is a clear and comprehensive definition of biblical counseling, was created through the cooperative effort of over thirty leading biblical counselors. The BCC has also published a three-part series of multi-contributor works that bring theological wisdom and practical expertise to pastors, church leaders, counseling practitioners, and students. Each year we are able to facilitate the production of numerous resources, including books, articles, videos, audio resources, and a host of other helps for biblical counselors. Working together allows us to provide robust resources and develop best practices in biblical counseling so that we can hone the ministry of soul care in the church.

To learn more about the BCC, visit biblicalcounselingcoalition.org.

Also from P&R Publishing on Overcoming Idolatry

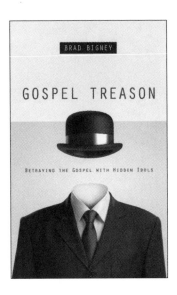

When we are struggling to grow in Christ, it's time to search our hearts for idolatry. Using personal examples, Bigney shows us how to recognize and root out hidden idols.

"Brad has thought a lot about the insidiousness of idolatry in today's culture. He has done a thorough job of showing us how modern-day idols are both offensive to God and grace-robbing to the believer. This book will cause you to consider your own heart in terms of what you really want and live for. It will also help you to minister to others who are suffering or caught in sin that hinders them from the freedom we have in the gospel."

—**Garrett Higbee**, President and Founder, Twelve Stones Ministries

From P&R Publishing on Toxic Marriages

God does not intend for marriage to be a place of oppression. Providing practical tools and exercises, biblical counselor Darby Strickland prepares potential helpers to pick up on cues that could point to abuse and to explore them wisely. You will learn how to identify a range of abusive behavior and better understand the impact of abuse on victims—particularly wives. Ultimately, you will become equipped to provide wise and Christ-centered counsel while navigating a difficult and complex situation.

"This resource and the wisdom it provides are integral to pastoral ministry—and indeed to the work of everyone who is ready to speak for the oppressed and cry out for justice. I cannot recommend it highly enough."
—**Rachael Denhollander**, Speaker; Author; Victim Advocate

Was this book helpful to you?
Consider writing a review online.
The author appreciates your feedback!

Or write to P&R at editorial@prpbooks.com
with your comments. We'd love to hear from you.